INTRODUCTION BY
BONNIE GREER

99
IMMIGRANTS
Who
MADE
BRITAIN
GREAT

LOUIS STEWART & NAOMI KENYON

INTRODUCTION BY
BONNIE GREER

99 IMMIGRANTS Who MADE BRITAIN GREAT

LOUIS STEWART & NAOMI KENYON

Canbury

First published by Canbury Press 2020
This edition published 2020

Canbury Press
Kingston upon Thames, Surrey, United Kingdom
Cover: Alice Marwick

Printed and bound in the UK by CPI Group (UK) Ltd, Croydon

This is a work of non-fiction.

Typeset by Canbury Press
in Minion and Gill Sans

ISBN
Hardback: 978-1-912454-33-4
Ebook: 978-1-912454-34-1
PDF: 978-1-912454-32-7

www.canburypress.com
Telling the real story since 2013

Dedicated to the immigrants who worked in the
NHS during the Covid-19 pandemic

Contents

Introduction

Over a decade ago now, I was invited to be a panellist on BBC TV's *Question Time*. Nick Griffin, then leader of the far-right British National Party, was also invited on as a guest. Then as now, the issue of immigration: good or bad, loomed large.

The British National Party claimed to be the party for 'indigenous Brits.' 'Indigenous' meaning 'native' to Britain. But one of the great joys is that your new country, the one that you choose and that in time chooses you, is always unfolding. This unfolding never stops.

This unfolding makes you eager to share with other citizens, pass on the gifts that you discover; those fascinating tidbits of history. And your own insight.

At the time of this particular Question Time, I was a Trustee of the British Museum. So I went to the Prehistory Department to ask about 'indigenous Brits.' I was told, by experts, that permafrost covered most of the British Isles, and that Southern Britain was a polar desert. And that the only thing 'indigenous' to Britain is... oats.

Therefore, everyone, every human being and animal, too, in the UK is descended from an immigrant. We are all incomers. Either yesterday. Or thousands of years ago.

In short, the UK is a nation of immigrants. The great Anglo Saxons, who gave the nation the English language, were Germano-Dutch. The Normans were from France by way of Scandinavia.

And so it goes on and on.

The Royal Family are German in origin. They changed their name from Saxe-Coburg and Gotha to that of their principal and favourite residence 'Windsor.' Immigration is the British history.

When I arrived in 1986, I found a nation steeped in a multicultural environment. No matter what other forces opposed to this reality wanted everyone to believe, this was a fact.

That immigrants have made a contribution to this nation is an understatement.

Immigrants are this nation.

Immigrants like the Olympic athlete, disability rights campaigner and television presenter Ade Adepitan. Born in Lagos, Nigeria, he was fifteen months old when polio made him unable to walk. His family moved to the UK when he was three and settled in London where Ade began playing wheelchair basketball. He played for Great Britain in the Paralympics. He was a member of the team that won the nation bronze in the 2004 Summer Paralympics and gold at the 2005 Paralympic World Cup.

Bushra Nasir was born in Pakistan and moved to England with her parents when she was eight years old. She had hoped to become a doctor and worked hard to earn herself a place. But her parents did not want her to leave London to study, so she took up biochemistry; then got a teaching degree; then took a teacher training course.

She worked for 15 years as a teacher; took up a headteacher's vacancy and became one of the first Muslim headteachers in the country. She raised her school's ratings and got many of her students into Cambridge and Oxford. But above all, she helped her students challenge racial and gender stereotypes. She has made them better students. Better citizens. And better human beings.

There are many, many stories of triumph like this in this book.

These stories show us the truth of the human spirit and the range of human courage. Immigrants not only enrich us, they bring a kind of insight that enables us all to reach beyond ourselves. Be more than ourselves.

Our very humanity is always in potential, always, in a sense, just beyond our reach. It appears at its strongest in moments of helping others. And also in those moments when we encounter 'the Other.' He or she who is different from us.

It is important for us here in Britain to know and understand this.

To understand that the tapestry of the land, its fabric, was created by immigrants. And that we grow, and rise, and thrive because of this fact.

From the Anglo Saxons who gave England its name; to the 17th century Huguenots who fled religious persecution in France and gave the English language the word 'refugee'; to Alf Dubs, listed here in this book – we are immigrants. Lord Dubs is a champion of refugee children who arrive in Europe and in Britain without their parents. Just as he did from his native Czechoslovakia, an unaccompanied Jewish child, on what was called, in 1939, the Kindertransport.

One of my real favourites listed here is John Edmonstone. Born into slavery in Guyana and named after his 'owner', Edmonstone's botany classes in Edinburgh in the 19th century were legendary. So legendary that the young Charles Darwin studied with him and was inspired to sail with *The Beagle* to South America. And into scientific and world history.

We now know that people of African descent lived and thrived in Tudor England. Shakespeare's immortal Dark Lady sonnets may have been inspired by one of these 'Black Tudors.'

The Bard writes in *Dark Lady*:

> The sea, all water, yet receives rain still,
> And in abundance addeth to his store;

Just as immigration does.

Because of it, we are made richer.

More abundant.

Flowing.

Bonnie Greer
Playwright and Commentator
Born in Chicago, USA

Author's Note

Our intention with this book is not to tell the stories of the featured individuals on their behalf or to introduce opinion; as two non-immigrants we have no right to do so. Instead, we have given a brief introduction to a small number of individuals who we hope readers will continue to familiarise themselves with and research further.

We started our research in the aftermath of the Brexit vote and the associated negative rhetoric about immigration. We felt ashamed that we were unaware of how many aspects of our modern British lives had been shaped – if not created – by immigrants, and how their experiences in life had moulded much of our everyday existence. To them, we are forever grateful.

Deciding who to include in this book has been challenging, to say the least. Our collection of biographies depicts only a fraction of those who have made Britain their home; there are a multitude of accounts we have not been able to feature. We encourage you to do some exploring and to make some discoveries of your own. It is also vital to note that by no means are we suggesting that immigrants are only welcome when they bring skills and value to Britain. However, we had to start somewhere and we did so with individuals who had a remarkable life story – that was well documented enough for us to research. The other criteria was diversity: none of the individuals were born in Britain and they come from all over the world. They are from all walks of life, and have followed a wide range of careers. We hope we have helped to represent the melting pot that is modern Britain. You may notice that there are slightly more men featured in the book than women. This reflects the imbalances we came across while researching: probably as a result of the historical objection to women in the workplace as well as a lack of documentation of women's pursuits.

Not only are these individual's journeys captivating, they are essential to understanding how contemporary Britain came to be. We hope that their stories will become known to all – tell everyone about them; from your kids to your grandparents! In doing so, we can ensure their incredible work is never drowned out by the ugly chorus in British public life which seeks to disparage and belittle immigrants.

If this book helps to undo some of that unpleasantness, it will have done its job.

We hope you find it as interesting to read as we did to research.

Louis Stewart and Naomi Kenyon

Ade Adepitan
Athlete and TV presenter

Ade Adepitan was born in Lagos, Nigeria. At 15 months old, he contracted polio which left him unable to walk. Aged three, his family moved to Britain and settled in London. At school, Ade showed a keen interest in becoming a sportsman and took up wheelchair basketball. Before long he was playing professionally for Great Britain. He won bronze at the 2004 Summer Paralympics in Athens and gold at the 2005 Paralympic World Cup in Manchester.

Ade's professionalism and personality won him fans in the media, leading him to present television programmes about sport and entertainment. He fronted later coverage of the Paralympic Games. He has also branched out into other formats, trekking through forests, deserts and mountains in Nicaragua with a team of people with disabilities for a documentary, *Beyond Boundaries*. He presented the prime-time BBC TV series *The Travel Show, New York: America's Busiest City, The World's Busiest Cities*, and *Africa with Ade Adepitan*.

Throughout his career, Ade has shown what can be achieved to other people with disabilities and to the general public. In particular, he has inspired the young black disabled community, and received a Certificate of Excellence from the Champions Club UK. In 2005, he was made an MBE for services to sport. He is patron of Go Kids Go, a charity that aims to help young wheelchair users with their skills and confidence and an ambassador for Right to Play, an organisation which teaches educational games to children in need.

Birthplace: Lagos, Nigeria
Born: 1973
Known For: Changing attitudes
towards disabled people

Alan Yau
Restaurateur

Alan Yau was born Yau Tak Wai in Hong Kong in 1962 and moved to join his family in Norfolk aged 12. He learnt how to run a food business while helping out his parents at their Chinese restaurant in Wisbech. He studied politics and philosophy at City of London Polytechnic and went into engineering and interior design. But food was in his blood and, in 1988, he started a takeaway business in Peterborough. Four years later he started the Wagamama restaurant chain, serving Japanese ramen on benches. The tangy flavours and canteen seating appealed and in 1997, he sold its 26 outlets for £60 million. So began a career which has changed Britain's taste buds.

In 1999, Alan started the Thai chain Busaba Eathai. In 2001, he founded the Hakkasan Chinese restaurant for high rollers in Mayfair, London, which won a Michelin star two years later. In 2004, he launched a contemporary dim sum tea house, Yauatcha. In 2008, he sold both Hakkasan and Yauatcha, and began an Italian bakery Princi UK, Babji, and the comfort food outlet Duck & Rice. Around this time, he was diagnosed with Bell's palsy, and left the UK for Thailand, where he trained to be a monk.

On returning to London, he launched Park Chinois, a palatial Chinese restaurant with a '1920s dance hall' vibe in a lavish rococo style with red velvet walls and golden candelabras. His latest venture is Softchow, a community-driven food discovery platform. He doesn't cook professionally, but devises concepts and dishes. He says that by the age of 70 (he is 57 at the time of writing), he would like to end his career in restaurants and begin spiritual and healing work.

Birthplace: Hong Kong
Born: 1962
Known For: Founding
Wagamama restaurant chain

Alec Issigonis
Car designer

In 1922 the Greco-Turkish War was ended by a catastrophic fire that engulfed the Greek city of Smyrna (today Izmir, Turkey). The Turkish forces regained control of the city and in the ensuing chaos of fire and persecution, tens of thousands of refugees fled the city in search of a new life. Among them was a young man, Alec Issigonis, and his two parents.

They were evacuated to Malta with the help of the British Royal Marines and eventually ended up in London, ready to start a new life. Alec studied engineering at Battersea Polytechnic and completed his education at the University of London. He entered the motor industry as a designer and engineer working for numerous different companies, including Humber, Austin, Alvis Cards and Morris Motors Limited.

Alec quickly made a name for himself and became known as 'the Greek God' by his colleagues and contemporaries for his groundbreaking work. His most famous creation is the Mini, which became known as the quintessentially British car due to its practicality and popularity with the working classes. Following further successes with the Morris Minor, Austin 1100, Austin 1800 and Austin Maxi, his work was recognised with several awards including an appointment as a CBE and a knighthood, making him a Sir. Alec retired from the motor industry in 1971 but his influence on the British motor industry has endured for generations.

Birthplace: Izmir, Turkey
Born: 1906 **Died:** 1988
Known For: Designing the Mini

Alek Wek
Model

Alek Wek was born in Sudan in 1977, the seventh of nine children. When civil war broke out in 1985, the family took refuge in the bush. They scavenged for food and found shelter in abandoned buildings, until they made their way to the capital Khartoum, where Alek's father died following a haemorrhage. From there, Alek's mother sent two of her daughters to London, hoping they would have a safer future.

Despite being unable to speak English, Alek committed herself to her education knowing that it would stand her in good stead for the future and gained a place at the London College of Fashion. She studied fashion business and technology but was soon discovered, on a day out in London, by a scout from a British model agency. Her career took off quickly as she began to model regularly, becoming the face of well-known luxury brands. She appeared in music videos for artists including Tina Turner and Janet Jackson and became recognised globally. Her success blazed a trail for dark-skinned women at a time when the industry was dominated by white faces.

Prominent black women including Oprah Winfrey and Lupita Nyong'o have praised Alek for changing perceptions of female attractiveness in Western society. As well as a glowing modelling career, she designed her own line of handbags titled Wek 1933 – an homage to the year of her father's birth. In 2002, she became an advisor to the US Refugees Advisory Council. She campaigns for greater awareness and support for refugees through her work with the United Nations Refugee Agency.

Birthplace: Wau, South Sudan
Born: 1977
Known For: Influencing
the fashion industry

Alf Dubs

Politician

Alf Dubs was born in Prague in 1932. His father was Jewish and the family fled Czechoslovakia when Germany invaded in 1938. He escaped to Britain on the Kindertransport, an effort to save Jewish children organised by the English stockbroker Sir Nicholas Winton. He was fortunate that his mother and father could meet him in Britain. Many other children of the Kindertransport never saw their parents again. Alf's experiences as a child, arriving alone at a place completely unknown to him, shaped his later life.

He studied at the London School of Economics, then worked briefly at the advertising agency Ogilvy & Mather before entering local government. In 1979, he was elected as a Labour MP for Battersea South. After a long career in public service, he became director of the Refugee Council. He also helped out at the civil rights organisation Liberty. In 1994, he was appointed as a Labour life peer.

In the House of Lords, Baron Dubs became alarmed by the rising number of immigrants arriving in Europe, the highest since World War Two. A quarter of the arrivals were said to be children. In 2016, Alf proposed an amendment to the Immigration Bill that would allow safe passage to these unaccompanied refugee children. The amendment was originally rejected, but accepted after another vote. Only 350 of the planned 3,000 children entered Britain, because the Home Office abandoned the scheme in 2017. Alf continues to campaign for refugees. He is a patron of Humanists UK and a trustee of the Immigration Advisory Service.

Birthplace: Prague, Czechia
Born: 1932
Known For: Campaigning
for the rights of child refugees

András Schiff
Pianist and conductor

András Schiff was born in Budapest, Hungary, to a Jewish family, the only child of two Holocaust survivors. He was immersed in music from a young age and studied at the Franz Liszt Academy of Music in Budapest, often winning piano competitions across Europe. He studied music in London with George Malcolm, a pianist and harpsichordist, and conducted a number of famous orchestras, including the London Philharmonic Orchestra and one he founded, Cappella Andrea Barca.

His interpretations of Mozart, Bach, Beethoven and Schubert have earnt him a worldwide following and his discography is renowned for its consistent excellence. For his solo performance of Bach, he received a Grammy Award in 1990. In 2014, he was knighted in the Queen's Birthday honours list for his services to music. He has been awarded the Mozart Medal, the Royal Academy of Music Bach Prize, and a gold medal by the Royal Philharmonic Society.

András lives in London, where he continues to play music. He is a vociferous opponent of anti-Semitism and racism in politics and society. He has been a persistent critic of the rise of far-right politics in Continental Europe. In 2011, he wrote to the *Washington Post* questioning whether his native Hungary should be given the presidency of the European Union. He refuses to return to the country of his birth because of the neo-fascist government of Viktor Orbán.

Birthplace: Budapest, Hungary
Born: 1953
Known For: Conducting
orchestras around the world

Anish Kapoor
Sculptor

Anish Kapoor was born in March 1954 in India. His father was a Punjabi Hindu and his mother an Iraqi Jew. After growing up in India he spent some time living on a kibbutz in Israel with his brother before moving to England to study art. While doing a postgraduate course at Chelsea College of Art, he was inspired by the work of Paul Neagu, a Romanian multi-media artist.

In the 1980s, Anish made mysterious pigment sculptures, geometric and organic, which appeared to have emerged from the walls or floor of the gallery. Whether working in stone, mirror, wax or PVC, his sculptures transform our perception of the material world. He has designed several architecturally scaled public artworks; notably Cloud Gate in Chicago's Millennium Park, Sky Mirror in Nottingham, Temenos in Middlesbrough, and Ark Nova, an inflatable concert hall created in the wake of the tsunami in Japan in 2011. In 2012, his 114 metre-high Orbit was unveiled at London's Olympic Games. It is Britain's largest piece of public art.

Anish's bold works have earned him multiple awards, including the Premio Duemila for Best Young Artist while representing Britain at the XLIV Venice Biennale in 1990, the Turner Prize in 1991, and India's prestigious Padma Bhushan Award in 2012. In 2013, he was knighted for services to the visual arts.

Birthplace: Mumbai, India
Born: 1954
Known For: Making giant works of art

Anna Freud
Psychoanalyst

Anna Freud was born in Vienna, Austria, to Martha Bernays and Sigmund Freud, the founder of psychoanalysis. Although born into a relatively comfortable family, she had a fraught relationship with her mother and sister, and developed severe eating disorders and depression. During these years, Anna was under the watchful eye of her father, whose diaries and letters are often said to analyse her behaviour and peculiarities. She was very close to her father and followed in his footsteps by beginning a career as a psychoanalyst.

When the Nazis occupied Austria, she moved to England with the rest of her family, aged 43. She continued her work in London, but whereas her father's work centred on the analysis of adults, she worked with children.

World War Two brought death and destruction to the lives of many young children in London. In the chaos, Anna with her colleague and close friend, Dorothy Burlingham, sought to create a place of safety for children and mothers where they could care for and educate their offspring. In 1941, they established the Hampstead War Nursery with the intention of analysing the impact of stress on children and their capacity to find substitute affections among peers in the absence of their parents. They later established the Hampstead Child Therapy Course and Clinic, which still exists today as the Anna Freud National Centre for Children and Families. Anna's pioneering work has led some to consider her, alongside Melanie Klein, as the founder of psychoanalytic child psychology.

Birthplace: Vienna, Austria-Hungary
Born: 1895 **Died:** 1982
Known For: Founding child psychoanalysis

Arthur Wharton
Footballer

Arthur Wharton was born in the Gold Coast in West Africa, in 1865. His mother was a member of the local Fante royalty and his father a Methodist Missionary from Grenada. Aged 19, Arthur moved to England to study theology. Instead, he discovered a love of sport and abandoned his education. Arthur excelled at football, but also shone at cricket, rugby and cycling. In 1886, he became the Amateur Athletics Association's sprint champion and was the first man to run 100 yards in 10 seconds.

Arthur became the first black footballer in the English football league and the world's first black professional football player when he kept goal for Darlington FC. Preston North End, the top club of the late 1880s, soon noticed his ability and he played for them for two years, before joining Rotherham Town and Sheffield United. Despite his prodigious skill, Arthur never won any major honours. He developed a drinking problem and his sporting career ended in 1902, playing for Stockport County in the second division.

Arthur became a coal miner, living in West Yorkshire with his wife Emma. He continued to play amateur cricket and reputedly ran fast enough to catch pigeons with his bare hands. He died in 1930 aged 65. Despite his sporting achievements, he was buried in an unmarked grave at Ellington Cemetery in Doncaster and largely forgotten until the 1980s. Anti-racism campaign groups finally secured a headstone in 1997. In 2003, Arthur's legacy was honoured posthumously with his induction into the English Football Hall of Fame. Nine decades after his death, statues of him stand in the FIFA headquarters in Zurich, Switzerland, and at St George's Park National Football Centre in the UK.

Birthplace: Jamestown, Gold Coast (now Ghana)
Born: 1865 **Died:** 1930
Known For: Being the first black professional footballer

Barbara Cooper
RAF officer

Barbara Cooper was born in Canada in 1958 and moved to Britain with her family when she was 11. After attending Evesham High School in Worcestershire, she joined the Women's Royal Air Force as an air-traffic controller. She was promoted to flight lieutenant and rose through the ranks in the 1980s. Her responsibilities included setting up and running the UK's Prisoner of War Information Bureau, which was tasked with finding British POWs. She also worked closely with the British and International Red Cross to develop ceremonies for servicemen and women killed in military operations around the world.

In 2008, Barbara made history when she was made an Air Commodore, becoming the highest-ranked female RAF officer. In 2010, she was put in charge of the Air Cadet Organisation, responsible for training more than 45,000 teenagers and 15,000 adult volunteers. In 2001, she was recognised for her work with her appointment as an Officer of the Order of the British Empire. Two years later, she received CBE in recognition of her service during the 2003 Iraq War.

In 2012, Barbara retired from full time service. She kept on working part time, dealing with service complaint appeals and acting as a trustee of the RAF Club.

Birthplace: Canada
Born: 1958
Known For: Rising to the top of the Royal Air Force

Bushra Nasir
Headteacher

Bushra Nasir, her siblings and mother moved from Pakistan to England to join her father. When she arrived aged eight, Bushra could not speak a word of English but was well supported by teachers and her family, who valued education. She failed the 11+ exam but passed the 13+ exam and went to grammar school. She had hoped to become a doctor and won a place to study medicine at the University of Birmingham, but when her parents were unhappy with her leaving London, she took a biochemistry degree instead and, later, a teacher training course nearer home. She worked for 15 years as a teacher in the school where she had been a pupil.

She then became a deputy head in an all-girls school in east London called Plashet. Most of its pupils came from low-income families and minority ethnicity backgrounds. After three years, Bushra was appointed headteacher in 1993 aged 40, becoming one of the first female Muslim headteachers in the country. During her 23 years at Plashet, she worked with staff and the community to transform it from an underachieving school into one rated 'outstanding' by Ofsted. Pupils were instilled with a sense of determination and self-worth, leading many to win places at leading universities such as Oxford and Cambridge.

Following the London tube bombings on 7 July 2005, Bushra was asked to advise the government on how to manage the wider impact of the terrorist attack on Britain's Muslim community. She was named Headteacher of the Year by the *Times Educational Supplement* in 2012, the year she retired from Plashet. She is currently chief executive of a multi-academy trust which runs four schools in Havering and mentors other headteachers.

Birthplace: Pakistan
Born: 1952
Known For: Transforming the lives of deprived pupils

Carlos Acosta
Ballet dancer

Carlos Acosta's family lived in deprivation in Havana, Cuba, when he was born in 1973, the youngest of 11 siblings. He spent much of his childhood outdoors where he would burn off his vast energy playing football with friends and exploring the mangrove swamps near his home, until his father, concerned that Carlos would get into trouble, decided his son would join the National Ballet School of Cuba.

Carlos was naturally talented and advanced quickly through his training under a number of world-class dancers and teachers. By the age of 16, he was performing internationally with multiple dance companies. He toured the world for two years, during which time he won gold at the Prix De Lausanne. A year later, he was invited to join the English National Ballet where he became its youngest ever lead dancer aged just 18.

Following his early success, Carlos moved to Texas where he joined the Houston Ballet and thrived, returning to England to join the Royal Ballet in 1998. He often took romantic roles. Since then, Carlos has reinforced his reputation as one of the world's greatest dancers, performing in as well as choreographing numerous high-profile shows with the Royal Ballet and starring as a guest dancer for other companies around the world. He was awarded a CBE in 2014 for his services to ballet. He retired from performing in 2016. He has focused on developing his own dance company and the Carlos Acosta International Dance Foundation, which trains young performers and choreographers.

Birthplace: Havana, Cuba
Born: 1973
Known For: Starring
at the Royal Ballet

Caroline Herschel
Astronomer

Caroline Lucretia Herschel was born in Hanover, Germany, in 1750, one of eight siblings. When she was 10, she fell ill with typhus which stunted her growth and damaged her eyesight. As a consequence, she was not expected to marry, and she spent her young life doing household chores, preparing her for a future as a maid. Following her father's death, however, Caroline ignored her mother's wishes and moved to Bath, England, in 1772 with her brother William, a professional musician whose hobby was astronomy.

Recognising Caroline's ability, William offered to tutor her in singing and mathematics. She began working as a singer, helping her brother with his star-gazing calculations in her spare time. As her astronomy improved, she made observations and discoveries of her own, including three new nebulae. In 1781, William discovered the planet Uranus, and was employed by King George III as a court astronomer. Recognising Caroline's contribution to her brother's work, the King employed her, too, in 1787, making her officially the world's first female astronomer.

Over the next 30 years, Caroline discovered eight new comets and 560 stars, cataloguing and presenting her findings and critiques of existing research to the Royal Society. Following William's death in 1822, she returned to Hanover and finalised the catalogues of their discoveries, an outstanding work for which she won the Astronomical Society's gold medal in 1828. She was awarded a gold medal for science by the King of Prussia before she passed away in Hanover, aged 97. She lives on in outer space in the names Asteroid *281 Lucretia* and moon crater *C. Herschel*.

Birthplace: Hanover, Germany
Born: 1750 **Died:** 1848
Known For: Discovering
hundreds of new stars

Charles Kao
Physicist and engineer

Charles Kao was born in Shanghai, China into a well-educated and respected family. His grandfather, Gao Xie, was a famous scholar and his father was a lawyer and professor. Charles was similarly well educated, moving between prestigious schools in China. He eventually moved to London to study at the University of Greenwich and did a PhD in electrical engineering at the University of London.

Charles began work at the Standard Telecommunication Laboratories where he was tasked with improving fibre optics. He quickly rose through the company and took over the whole optical communications programme in 1964. His most notable piece of work was the development of cables containing ultra-pure glass that could transmit light over long distances with minimal loss of signal. This discovery laid the foundation for the evolution of the internet and Charles' influential work is widely recognised as essential to its development.

Charles spent the remainder of his life moving between China, the United States and Britain, working and teaching at the Chinese University of Hong Kong, Yale University and Imperial College London. He died in Hong Kong in 2018. He is known as the 'Godfather of Broadband'.

Birthplace: Shanghai, China
Born: 1933 **Died:** 2018
Known For: Developing fibre optics that carry the internet

Charles Yerkes
Financier

Born in 1837, Charles Yerkes was a highly successful financier from Philadelphia, USA, who was instrumental in building one of London's most famous features. Starting out at 17, Charles began as a broker and quickly progressed through the ranks of finance in Philadelphia, until his career was abruptly halted by a stock market scandal: he was jailed for larceny. On his release, Yerkes turned his attention to Chicago's railway industry. A series of takeovers left him owning the majority of the city's public railway system as well as a dubious reputation. In 1899, Yerkes sold his interests in Chicago and started collecting art in New York.

In 1900, he abruptly changed direction again and sailed for England. At the time, the future of London's public railway service was uncertain. Funding was falling, but the city was growing. Charles saw an opportunity and used his experience in Chicago to start a new venture, the Underground Electric Railways Company of London. The money he raised funded the digging of the Tube's three deepest lines — the Northern, Piccadilly and Bakerloo. It also paid for the construction of Lots Road Power Station in Chelsea, which powered the underground network until its closure in 2002.

Charles died in 1905 after a battle with kidney disease, just five years after arriving in London. Months later, the Northern, Piccadilly and Bakerloo Lines opened to the public, allowing passengers to hurtle along almost 200 feet under the streets. Londoners still benefit daily from an American's entrepreneurial zeal. In 2016-17, 573 million journeys were undertaken on the three lines he built.

Birthplace: Philadelphia, USA
Born: 1873 **Died:** 1905
Known For: Building the
London Underground

Charlotte Auerbach
Geneticist

Charlotte Auerbach was born in 1899 in Krefeld, Germany, to a Jewish family of eminent scientists. After studying chemistry and biology at university, she went into teaching, but was dismissed after a few years for being Jewish. When Adolf Hitler took power in 1933, she moved to Scotland and studied at the University of Edinburgh.

In Edinburgh, she worked with Hermann Joseph Muller, a Nobel laureate whose work and ethos she admired. Hermann was known for his pioneering research into the genetic effects of radiation and Charlotte followed in his footsteps as a campaigner against nuclear weapons. She began conducting experiments into the genetic effects of mustard gas, a poison sprayed on troops in World War One. She found how the gas mutated genes – but was told not to publish her work by the government because of the outbreak of World War Two. Her research was finally published in 1947, the same year that she became a lecturer at the University of Edinburgh.

Her work helped to establish the science of mutagenesis, when genes are changed naturally or by a physical or chemical element. In 1976, she received the Royal Society's Darwin Medal, in recognition of her significant contribution to biology, though her most prized award was said to be a letter from Hermann congratulating her on her discoveries. She lived in Edinburgh with her two adopted sons, both immigrants themselves from Germany and Italy, until her death in 1989, aged 90. To this day there still exists a road in Edinburgh and a building at the Royal Society of Edinburgh named after her.

Birthplace: Krefeld, Germany
Born: 1899 **Died:** 1989
Known For: Discovering how
chemical warfare affects victims

Claudia Jones
Journalist and activist

Claudia Jones was born in Belmont, Port of Spain, Trinidad. At the age of nine, her family moved to Harlem in the United States. Shortly after their arrival, her mother died, throwing the Joneses deeper into poverty. While Claudia was a gifted student, she was forced to abandon her studies and take up work. In 1932, she was diagnosed with tuberculosis, which dogged her for the rest of her life. Despite her difficulties, Claudia spent her young life fighting for racial equality. As well as writing and editing political magazines, she became a member and then a leader of the Communist Party. Arrested as part of the McCarthyite 'reds under the bed' witch-hunt, she was deported to Britain in 1955.

On arrival, Claudia settled in London and deployed the activism that she had honed in America and fought racism towards the British African-Caribbean community. She campaigned against its manifestation in education, employment, housing and laws that restricted non-white migration to Britain. She founded and edited the *West Indian Gazette,* which gave her community a voice. In 1958, her response to a series of racially motivated riots in Notting Hill had a long-lasting impact. She began a 'Caribbean Carnival' inside St Pancras Town Hall to celebrate Caribbean culture. Now held outside, the Notting Hill Carnival has run every year since, attracting hundreds of thousands of people.

At the age of just 49, Claudia died of a heart attack and tuberculosis and was buried next to Karl Marx in Highgate Cemetery. She is recognised as one of the greatest black Britons.

Birthplace: Belmont, Trinidad
Born: 1915 **Died:** 1964
Known For: Founding the
Notting Hill Carnival

Claus Moser
Statistician

Claus Moser was born in Berlin, Germany, in 1922 to an educated and musical Jewish family, who emigrated to England when they were displaced by the rise of Nazism. He thrived at Frensham Heights School in Surrey. He was a skilled pianist and chorister, but in 1940, after the fall of France during World War Two, he, his brother and his father were deemed 'friend enemy aliens' and interned in Liverpool. There, while mixing with many other learned internees, he developed a love of statistics and later studied the subject at the London School of Economics. After he graduated, he joined the RAF as a mechanic.

In 1946, he returned to the London School of Economics as an assistant lecturer in statistics and, in 1961, became Professor of Social Statistics. When his work caught the attention of Prime Minister Harold Wilson, he was appointed to head the Central Statistics Office. He improved the reliability of economic data, often winning over those in power to his point of view. He was behind the influential annual report tracking changes in British society, *Social Trends*. And he encouraged the publication of national statistics to the public.

A lover of the arts, Claus was passionate about the importance of culture in British society. His chairmanship of the subsidised Royal Opera House between 1974 and 1987 is often credited with ensuring its survival under Margaret Thatcher's government. His outstanding work was formally recognised in 2001 when he was made Baron Moser of Regents Park. He died in 2015 following a stroke while on holiday in Switzerland, surrounded by his friends and family. He was 92.

Birthplace: Berlin, Germany
Born: 1922 **Died:** 2015
Known For: Popularising
government statistics

Connie Mark
Campaigner

Connie Mark was born in Kingston, Jamaica, in 1923. One grandparent hailed from India, another from Scotland, and one was part Lebanese. Jamaica was a British colony at the time and, despite their diverse ancestry, the Marks family considered themselves to be British. Aged 19, Connie joined the Auxiliary Territorial Service, the women's branch of the British Army, where she served for 10 years. She experienced racial prejudice and was repeatedly denied pay rises. Nonetheless, she served with distinction and became a full corporal. Her commanding officer nominated her for a British Empire Medal – but it was turned down.

Connie eventually moved to Britain after Stanley Goodridge, her cricketing husband, won a contract to play for Durham. She worked as a medical secretary. In her spare time, spurred on by her experiences at the Auxiliary Territorial Service, she campaigned for racial and women's equality.

In 1980, Connie founded Friends of Mary Seacole, later named the Mary Seacole Memorial Association, to recognise the accomplishments of the black Crimean War nurse and, in 1993, the British government set up an award in Mary Seacole's name. Feeling that their role had been underplayed or in some cases ignored entirely, Connie lobbied for the inclusion and representation of black Britons on war memorials. In 1992, she finally received the British Empire Medal and, in 2001, was awarded an OBE. In 2007, she suffered a heart attack and died. In 2008, the Nubian Jak Community Trust erected a blue plaque in her memory on Mary Seacole House.

Birthplace: Kingston, Jamaica
Born: 1923 **Died:** 2007
Known For: Campaigning
for racial equality

Deborah Doniach
Immunologist

Deborah Doniach was born in Switzerland in 1912, and became a pioneering medical researcher. Her father was a well-respected pianist and her mother founded a dance school in Paris, but Deborah did not want to follow in their footsteps. Instead, she studied medicine in Paris, and at the Royal Free Medical School in London. She worked as a junior doctor and surgeon for London County Council before moving to Middlesex Hospital, where she was an endocrinologist in the department of chemical pathology.

In the 1950s, her career took off when she studied glands and made a number of acute observations about cell and antibody behaviour. With her fellow researchers Ivan Roitt and Peter Campbell, she helped to further the understanding of the thyroid gland's role in immunity and disease, leading to the recognition of organ-specific autoimmunity – a discovery that has saved countless lives.

In the 1960s, Deborah joined the newly created department of immunology at Middlesex Hospital, where she became a professor. Throughout her career, she made significant discoveries about the autoimmune response of various parts of the body to disease. Like many researchers, she pursued her academic interest deep into her retirement, writing her final immunological review at the age of 91, shortly before she died in London in 2004. She and her husband Sonny had been together for 75 years by the time of his death in 2001.

Birthplace: Geneva, Switzerland
Born: 1912 **Died:** 2004
Known For: Pioneering research into autoimmune diseases

Dennis Gabor
Physicist and engineer

Dennis Gabor was born in 1900 to a Jewish family in Budapest, Hungary. After World War One, he studied at the Technische Hochschule in Berlin, where he received a diploma in electrical engineering and, later, a doctorate. In 1933, like many other Jews in Germany, he decided to settle in Britain.

Dennis started working as a scientist at the British Thomson-Houston engineering company in Rugby, Warwickshire. His experiments were intended to improve electron microscopes but, in 1947, he unexpectedly invented the hologram. A hologram is a three-dimensional image formed by the interference of light beams from a laser. Holograms have many modern uses, including in art, data storage and security on banknotes. Dennis became known as the 'Father of Holography.'

But it was not the limit of his talents. His investigations laid the groundwork for the theory of granular synthesis which was key to developing time-frequency analysis in signal processing, a field of electrical engineering. He became Professor of Applied Electron Physics at Imperial College and was garlanded with awards. In 1956, he was elected a Fellow of the Royal Society and in 1970 received a CBE. But the biggest accolade came in 1971 when he received the Nobel Prize in Physics for 'his invention and development of the holographic method'. After his retirement, Dennis continued his connection with Imperial College and worked on many projects. He died in London aged 78.

Birthplace: Budapest, Hungary
Born: 1900 **Died:** 1979
Known For: Inventing holographs

Dietrich Küchemann
Engineer

Dietrich Küchemann was born in Göttingen, Germany. His mother came from a long line of musicians and his father was a devoted schoolteacher. Dietrich studied aerodynamics at the University of Göttingen, where he worked with Ludwig Prandtl, a pioneer of aerodynamic science and design. At the outbreak of World War Two, Dietrich offered his service but was not drafted. Instead, he and his colleague Johanna Weber researched jet engines and flight. In 1945, Dietrich's study area was occupied by the British, who continued to fund his work. In 1946, he and Johanna moved to Britain to work for UK science.

In 1953, Dietrich became a British citizen and eventually chief scientific officer and head of the aerodynamics department at the Royal Aircraft Establishment in Farnborough, Surrey. While there, he helped design the delta wing, later used on the Eurofighter Typhoon and Concorde. He also developed an anti-shock body – known as a 'Küchemann carrot'– that reduced drag once an aircraft travelled close to the speed of sound. He was awarded the Royal Aeronautical Society's Silver Medal, made a fellow of the Royal Society, and appointed a CBE.

Up until his death in 1976, Dietrich worked to improve aerodynamics. His work is cited as instrumental to the development and improvement of high-speed travel. His book, *The Aerodynamic Design of Aircraft*, is still used today to understand the mechanics of flight.

Birthplace: Göttingen, Germany
Born: 1911 **Died:** 1976
Known For: Developing
high-speed flight

Doreen Lawrence
Campaigner

Doreen Lawrence was born in 1952 in Jamaica and moved to Britain when she was nine. She worked in a bank in the city and married Neville Lawrence, a painter and decorator, in 1972. They had three children, Stephen, Stuart and Georgina. Stephen wanted to be an architect. On 22 April 1993, he was brutally murdered in a racially motivated attack while waiting for a bus in Eltham. Five suspects were arrested for the killing but none was charged. The case became notorious.

Doreen and Neville maintained that the police investigation was poorly conducted as a result of racism and incompetence. In 1999, a public inquiry concluded that the initial investigation by the Metropolitan Police had been botched and that the force was 'institutionally racist'. Doreen and her husband kept up the public pressure on police to find the culprits responsible for their son's death. In 2011, following new genetic testing of hair and blood samples, two of the original suspects stood trial for Stephen's murder and, one year later, were found guilty.

Doreen continues to campaign tirelessly for racial justice and equality. In 1998, she set up the Stephen Lawrence Charitable Trust to help people aged 13 to 30 from disadvantaged backgrounds and to build communities. Among its wide-ranging work, it has given 130 bursaries to young people to become architects. In 2003, Doreen was awarded an OBE for services to community relations. In 2013, she was made Baroness Lawrence of Clarendon. She sits on the Labour benches in the House of Lords.

Birthplace: Jamaica
Born: 1952
Known For: Campaigning
for justice for her son

Edith Bülbring
Scientist

Edith Bülbring was born in 1903 in Bonn, Germany, and studied medicine there and in Munich and Freiburg. She started research under the pharmacologist Ulrich Friedemann, but he was dismissed from his position by the Nazis because he was Jewish. Jews were barred from working in universities or the professions. Edith also had Jewish heritage, and in 1933 travelled to England with her two sisters.

Edith became assistant to a professor of pharmacology at the University of Oxford. She was fascinated by smooth muscle. Smooth muscle is a type of elastic cell found throughout the body, found in veins and arteries and in hollow organs such as the stomach, bladder and uterus, among other places. Intrigued by its unpredictability, she specialised in the study of this neglected field for the remainder of her career. She built up a large research group of colleagues on smooth muscle and was the most influential researcher working in the area. Her work focussed on the role played by neurotransmitters.

Edith received two of the highest accolades in her field – the Wellcome Gold Medal in Pharmacology and the German Pharmacological Society's Schmiedeberg-Plakette, its greatest honour. She retired in 1971, but continued casual work at the Physiology Laboratory in Oxford. After experiencing circulation problems in one of her feet, one leg was amputated and she died in 1990.

Birthplace: Bonn, Germany
Born: 1903 **Died:** 1990
Known For: Leading research into smooth muscle

Emma Orczy
Novelist and playwright

Emmuska Orczy (later known as Emma) was born in Hungary in 1865 into an upper-class family, the daughter of a well-known composer and a countess who moved around European cities. Fearing a working-class revolution would take place in Hungary, Emma's parents moved the family to London when she was 14.

Emma attended West London School of Art and Heatherley School of Fine Art, where she met her future husband, the illustrator Montague MacLean Barstow. Following the birth of their only child in 1899, Emma worked as a writer and translator. She had only modest success until, in 1903, she came up with the idea for an appealing short story. *The Scarlet Pimpernel* recounted with swashbuckling verve the secret double life of a foppish Englishman, Sir Percy Blakeney, who rescued members of the aristocracy from execution during the French Revolution. While book publishers considered publishing the story as a novel, it was accepted as a stage play and debuted at the New Theatre in London's West End in 1905. *The Scarlet Pimpernel* quickly became a box office sensation, performed more than 2,000 times on the stage and translated into multiple languages.

Emma wrote many more short stories and novels, including *I Will Repay* and *The Old Man in the Corner*, as well as an autobiography. But she will always be best known for *The Scarlet Pimpernel*. It has been repeatedly revived and adapted for stage, screen and radio. Following a period spent in Monte Carlo during the Second World War, Emma returned to England and died in Henley on Thames in 1947. She was 82.

Birthplace: Tarnaörs, Hungary
Born: 1865 **Died:** 1947
Known For: Writing
The Scarlet Pimpernel

Erich Reich
Entrepreneur

Erich Reich was born in Vienna, Austria in 1935, and deported to Poland by the Nazis during World War Two when he was three. One year later, he and his elder brothers were rescued by the Kindertransport programme and taken to London. His parents were sent to Auschwitz concentration camp, where they died.

Erich spent most of his childhood with his foster family in Surrey, before attending a Jewish school in north London. When he was 13, he went to live with his aunt and uncle in Israel, where he stayed until adulthood, serving in the Israeli army. On returning to England, he began working for Thompson Holidays, where was promoted to operations director. He moved to the rival tour operator Thomas Cook and became its managing director in 1979. Eight years later, he established Classic Tours, a global charity fundraising company that hosted outdoors challenges overseas including cycling, horse-riding and mountain climbing events. Its first bike ride raised more than £600,000. Classic Tours has raised more than £60 million for 300 different charities, with the support and involvement of 42,000 people.

Erich was knighted for services to charity in 2010. As well as raising vast amounts of money for good causes, he has continued to be involved in efforts to remember the Kindertransport that saved his life and those of 10,000 other refugee children during the war.

Birthplace: Vienna, Austria
Born: 1935
Known For: Raising
£60 million for charity

Ernst Chain

Scientist

Ernst Chain was born in 1906 in Berlin, Germany, into a Jewish family. His father was a chemist and industrialist. From an early age Ernst was interested in his father's work and studied chemistry at university in Berlin. With the Nazis' rise to power in the 1930s, he was no longer welcome in his homeland. He moved to Britain in 1933 and began working at University College Hospital, London. He later became a student at the University of Cambridge and then a lecturer at the University of Oxford.

During World War Two, Ernst and an Australian colleague at Oxford, Howard Florey, began to investigate the effects of substances produced by micro-organisms and their antibacterial properties. They researched penicillin, which had been accidentally discovered two decades earlier by the Scottish doctor Alexander Fleming at his laboratory in St. Mary's Hospital, London. Ernst and Florey managed to purify penicillin, concentrating its germ-killing properties.

In 1945, Ernst, Howard and Alexander won the Nobel Prize for Physiology or Medicine for the development of penicillin, which is estimated to have saved more than 200 million lives – four times the number of deaths in World War Two. When the war was over, Ernst discovered that his mother and sister had perished in Nazi concentration camps. He moved to Rome to work at the Istituto Superiore di Sanità. He returned to Britain in 1964, to found the biochemistry department at Imperial College, where he worked until his retirement. In 1969, he was knighted by Queen Elizabeth II. A few years later, he was appointed a fellow of the Royal Society. He died in 1979, aged 73.

Birthplace: Berlin, Germany
Born: 1906 **Died:** 1979
Known For: Developing an antibiotic
that has saved 200 million lives

Ernst Gombrich
Author

Ernst Gombrich was born in Vienna, Austria-Hungary, into an upper-class family of Jewish ancestry. The Gombrichs were acquainted with notable musicians, writers and artists, exposing their son to high culture and society from a young age. He studied art history at Vienna University with an influential founder of modern art, Julius von Schlosser, among other art historians. In 1939, he fled the Nazis and moved to Britain to work as a researcher at the University of London. During World War Two, he worked for the BBC translating German radio for British intelligence. He broke the news of Adolf Hitler's death to Winston Churchill.

After the war, Ernst returned to the University of London, where he became director of the Warburg Institute in 1959, and rekindled his passion, the study of cultural history. He began working on a book that would soon become *The Story of Art*. Published in 1950, *The Story of Art* has sold over seven million copies, making it the highest selling art book of all time. This and many other works, such as *Art and Illusion*, *Meditations on a Hobby Horse*, and *Aby Warburg: An Intellectual Biography*, have led him to be hailed as 'one of the most influential scholars and thinkers of the 20th century.'

In 1947, he became a British citizen and in 1966 he was appointed an OBE. Six years later, he was made a Knight Bachelor, becoming Sir Ernst Gombrich. His work has informed numerous prominent thinkers and remains to this day one of the best introductions to the visual arts, engaging students across Britain and the world.

Birthplace: Vienna, Austria-Hungary
Born: 1909 **Died:** 2001
Known For: Writing
The Story of Art

Eugène Rimmel
Perfumer

Eugène Rimmel was born in France, the son of a perfume maker, who taught his son how to make exquisite scents. Eugène moved to London, where he opened a perfume shop, The House of Rimmel, on Bond Street in 1834. He became an expert in manufacturing products and supplied high society with his scents, make-up and hygiene products, earning him the title of 'The Prince of Perfumers'.

Eugène's shop was popular with high-profile and influential customers including Queen Victoria, who employed Eugène as her personal perfumer. He is believed to have travelled the world to develop his products and experimented with scents and colours that had not been seen before. His best-known items were perfumes, fragranced pomades, cosmetics, mouth rinses and mascara.
Each product was beautifully packaged and some bore the Royal Warrant stamp of approval, highlighting another of Eugène's skills – marketing. He understood that the popularity of his products in the upper classes would morph into the mass market and developed advertisements and stylish catalogues to sell to the wider public.

In 1887, Eugène died and the store was passed to his family and was eventually bought up by Coty, Inc. Today Rimmel London is one of Britain's best-known cosmetics brands, with some of its lines endorsed by the supermodel Kate Moss.

Birthplace: France
Born: 1820 **Died:** 1887
Known For: Founding
The House of Rimmel

Fanny Eaton
Model

Fanny Entwhistle (later Eaton) was born in Jamaica in 1835 to a previously enslaved mother. Her father's identity remains unknown. At some point during her youth, Fanny was brought to London by her mother and met her husband James, with whom she had 10 children.

Fanny was beautiful. In her twenties, she began to sit regularly as an artist's model at the Royal Academy for a number of painters, starting with Simeon Solomon, whose 1860 work *The Mother of Moses* featuring her was exhibited at the Royal Academy. Members of the Pre-Raphaelite Brotherhood, a collective of English artists, were impressed with Fanny and regularly chose her as a muse for their paintings. Dante Gabriel Rosetti praised her beauty and depicted her in one of his most iconic paintings, *The Beloved,* in 1865. While Fanny usually featured as a number of different characters in paintings, her own portrait, *The Head of Mrs Eaton,* was painted by Joanna Bryce in 1861.

Fanny's time as a muse is thought to have ended after 10 years, as a result of the death of her husband and her commitments to her large family. She spent her latter years working as a seamstress and cook on the Isle of Wight, but returned to London and her family before her death in 1924. While the time she spent modelling was short, her work is historically and culturally significant in its subversion of the societal norms and the beauty standards of Victorian London. Fanny often appeared as the central focus of the paintings she modelled for. Previously women of colour had been treated as an accessory to the beauty of white women.

Birthplace: St. Andrew Parish, Jamaica
Born: 1935 **Died:** 1924
Known For: Modelling for the Pre-Raphaelites

Freddie Mercury
Pop singer

Farrokh Bulsara was born in Stone Town in the British protectorate of
Zanzibar but spent most of his childhood in India. There, he developed
a love of music, studied piano at school and started a band, *The Heretics*,
who played rock and roll. In 1963, he returned home to his parents in
Zanzibar with a love of Western pop music and a new first name, Freddie.

In 1964, when a revolution overthrew the Sultan of Zanzibar and
thousands died, Freddie's family fled Africa for the west London suburb
of Feltham. Freddie began studying graphic art and design at Ealing Art
College during which time he befriended a drummer, Roger Taylor and
a guitarist, Brian May. They were already in a band called *Smile*. Freddie
replaced the lead singer and changed the band's name to *Queen* and his
own surname to Mercury. A bassist, John Deacon, joined the group in
1971. Queen went on to become one of the bestselling pop bands of all
time, selling an estimated 300 million records. Freddie's vocal range and
flamboyant on-stage persona turned him into one of the greatest singers
in history.

In 1991, Freddie died of AIDS, aged 45. As one of its most famous
victims, his death raised the awareness of the disease. His fellow *Queen*
band members set up the Mercury Phoenix Trust in his name. To date, it
has given away £17 million and funded more than 1,000 projects fighting
HIV and AIDS. *Queen's* songs continue to delight audiences around the
world. Freddie's life and achievements were celebrated in the 2018 film,
Bohemian Rhapsody.

Birthplace: Zanzibar
Born: 1946 **Died:** 1991
Known For: Writing
and singing *Queen's* songs

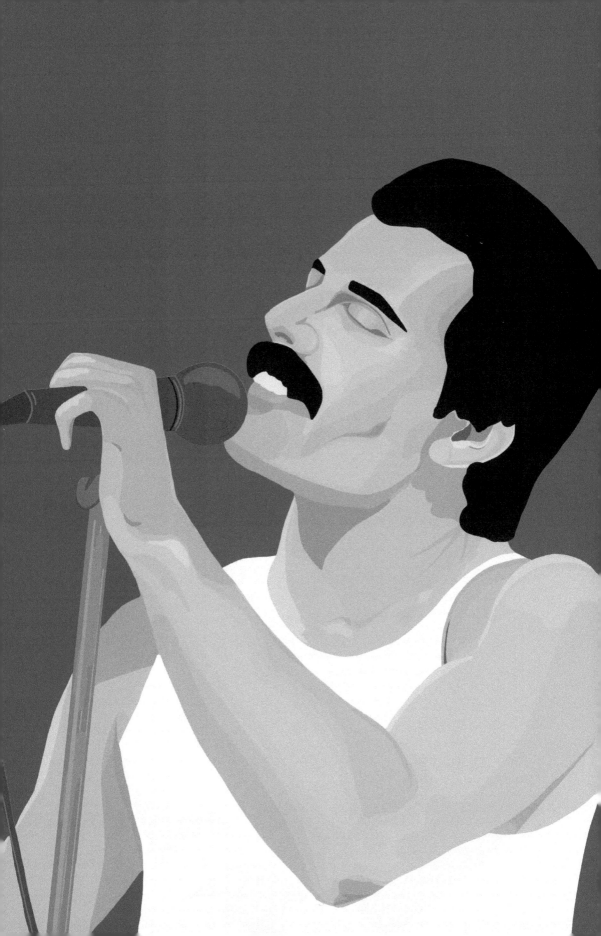

George Frideric Handel
Composer

George Frideric Handel was born in 1865 in Halle-upon-Saale, a part of Brandenburg-Prussia. His love of music took hold from an early age, though his father, a coppersmith, did not approve: he tried to stop him owning any musical instruments. Finding a more empathetic ally in his mother, George nurtured his talent learning to play the violin, and later joined an opera orchestra. Under the tuition of Frederic Wilhelm Zachow, a renowned German musician and composer, he studied the organ, the oboe, harpsichord and violin, increasingly convinced that – whether his father approved or not – he would dedicate his life to music.

In 1712, he settled in England and had his first big success with his opera Rinaldo, the first Italian language opera written for the London stage. He had admirers in high places, and regularly performed for King George I and Queen Anne, for which he received an annual allowance of £200 a year, a vast sum at the time. In 1727, he became a British subject, earning him the right to compose music for the Chapel Royal, for which he wrote the Coronation Anthem for George II and the Funeral Anthem for Queen Caroline. In 1741, he composed one of the most performed choral works of all time, *The Messiah*. In 1749, he composed *Music for the Royal Fireworks*, a celebration held in Green Park to mark the end of the War of the Austrian Succession. A year later, he held another opera to benefit the Foundling Hospital, which was set up to help with the 'education and maintenance of exposed and deserted young children'.

Considered to be the greatest composer of the baroque era, George remained in London until his death in 1759. He was given a full state funeral, and rests in Westminster Abbey.

Birthplace: Halle, Germany
Born: 1865 **Died:** 1759
Known For: Composing
The Messiah

George Weidenfeld
Publisher

The future publishing magnate was born in 1919 to a Jewish family in Vienna, the capital of Austria. After attending university there, his family was forced to leave when the Nazis annexed the country. George settled in Britain and, with the aid of the British Jewish community, was able to establish a place in society.

He spent several years at the BBC as a political commentator before turning his hand to book publishing in 1949, co-founding a book publisher with the British politician Nigel Nicolson, Weidenfeld & Nicolson. The company's success was predicated on some bold decisions, for instance daring to publish Vladimir Nabokov's *Lolita*, a controversial bestseller in 1955. In its early years, it also published other notable works: non-fiction by the historian Hugh Trevor-Roper and the philosopher Isaiah Berlin and fiction by the American novelist Saul Bellow. In 1993, George arranged the publication of a book by John Paul II, *Memory and Identity*.

The company was later sold to the Orion Publishing Group, but George remained an engaged philanthropist and businessman (he was frequently referred to as a 'master networker'), and he worked to promote better diplomatic relations between various countries, among them Britain, France and Germany. A British citizen since 1947, he was later appointed a life peer, taking the title of Baron Weidenfeld of Chelsea. He died in 2016, aged 96.

Birthplace: Vienna, Austria
Born: 1919 **Died:** 2016
Known For: Founding publisher
Weidenfeld & Nicolson

Gina Miller
Entrepreneur and activist

Gina Miller was born in 1965 in British Guiana. At the age of 10, she was sent by her parents to school in Eastbourne, East Sussex. While at school she worked in hotels and restaurants, before studying first law, and then marketing at university. She began working as a marketer, first for BMW, and then launched her own financial services marketing agency. In 2009, she and her husband, Alan Miller, co-founded the investment firm, SCM Direct. The same year, she set up the True and Fair Foundation, a charity aiming to limit future mis-selling and financial scandals through greater transparency.

When the United Kingdom voted for Brexit in June 2016, Gina hired a law firm, Mishcon de Reya, to challenge the British Government's decision to leave the European Union without obtaining the permission of Parliament. In November 2016, the High Court ruled in her favour, giving MPs the final say over the withdrawal, which they duly approved. In 2019, Gina and a number of others challenged the Government for a second time arguing that Boris Johnson's sudden suspension of Parliament was unconstitutional. In September 2019, the Supreme Court unanimously found in their favour, forcing Parliament to be re-established.

Gina's success came at a cost. She encountered racist and sexist abuse and death threats, which led to several arrests. In 2017, she was named by Powerlist as the 'UK's most influential black person.'

Birthplace: British Guiana
Born: 1965
Known For: Asserting
the rights of Parliament

Graeme Hick
Cricketer

Born in Rhodesia (now Zimbabwe) in 1966, to tobacco farming parents, the future professional cricketer Graeme Hick gravitated towards his chosen sport early in life. He played for local school teams, and later became the youngest ever player to be picked for the Zimbabwean World Cup squad in 1983.

He left his hometown for England the following year after receiving a scholarship to play cricket for Worcestershire, where he would spend the rest of his 24 year career, and amass the bulk of his 40,000 first-class runs. During his time there, Graham played internationally for the England team, and made his debut as a batsman against the West Indies in 1991, helping the team reach the World Cup Final a year later, and topping both batting and bowling averages in England's tour of India in 1993. He was one of England's star players throughout the early 1990s, and accumulated high batting averages in test matches against South Africa and the West Indies, eventually achieving second place in the world rankings.

In 2008, at the age of 42, Graeme retired from professional cricket, by which stage he had surpassed the record for the most cricket matches played, 1,214 – still a global record – and accumulated 64,000 first-class runs, including 136 centuries. He is one of only 25 players to have scored more than 100 first-class hundreds, and retired an England legend.

Birthplace: Harare, Zimbabwe
Born: 1966
Known For: Playing the most cricket matches in history

Hans Holbein
Painter

In 1497, Hans Holbein the Younger was born into an artistic family in the free imperial city of Augsburg, in what is now Bavaria. His father was an accomplished painter and draughtsman, skills he passed onto Hans and his brother Ambrosius. Hans' skill as an artist was recognised early and it soon gave him a living. He spent much of his life travelling from one country to the next, painting, illustrating, woodcutting and occasionally designing stained-glass windows. One of his most notable works includes the title page of Martin Luther's Bible.

He moved to England in 1526, employed by Sir Thomas More with the help of a recommendation from Erasmus, during which time he painted what would go on to become his celebrated *Portrait of Sir Thomas More*. Returning home now comparatively wealthy, he was soon back in England. He had become an associate of Thomas Cromwell and the Boleyn family, both of whom helped him find work, and he eventually became a court painter for Henry VIII. During this time he painted *The Ambassadors*, which remains on display in the National Gallery in London. His later painting of Henry VIII is widely considered one of the most iconic images of the King, though it was destroyed by fire in 1698.

Hans remained in London until his death in 1543, by all accounts a victim of the plague. He left behind him a body of work that secured his legacy.

Birthplace: Augsburg, Germany
Born: 1497 **Died:** 1543
Known For: Painting the
court of Henry VIII

Hans Krebs
Scientist

The biologist, physician and biochemist Hans Krebs was born in 1900 in Hildesheim, Germany, into a family of Jewish-Silesian ancestry. Inspired by his father's career as a surgeon, he studied at a number of prestigious German universities and developed a particular interest in medical research. With his fellow researcher Kurt Henseleit, he identified a biochemical reaction that takes place in the liver to produce urea from ammonia, known as the 'urea cycle'. This was the first metabolic cycle to be identified, and came to be known as the Krebs-Henseleit cycle.

When the Nazis rose to power during the 1930s, Hans fled Germany and arrived at the University of Cambridge. Under the guidance of Sir Frederick Gowland Hopkins, a renowned Noble prize-winning biologist, he settled into Cambridge life, and in 1934 became demonstrator in biochemistry. A year later, he took up a lecturing position at the University of Sheffield, where he further developed the work that he had begun in Germany years previously. With his colleague William Johnson, he began research that led to the discovery of the 'citric acid cycle', the process by which organisms release stored energy from carbohydrates, fats and proteins.

In 1953, Hans received the Nobel Prize in Physiology or Medicine for the discovery of this cycle, which came to be named after him: the Hans Cycle. He was knighted in 1958, and spent the rest of his career at the University of Oxford. He died in 1981, aged 81. The University of Oxford eventually demolished its Hans Krebs Tower, but the University of Sheffield still has a Krebs Institute of bio-molecular research.

Birthplace: Hildesheim, Germany
Born: 1900 **Died:** 1981
Known For: Discovering the Hans Cycle

Harry Gordon Selfridge
Retailer

The future owner of the celebrated British department stores was born in Wisconsin, USA, in 1858. Harry's father had left the family after fighting in the American Civil War, leaving him with his two older brothers in the care of their mother. After the early death of both his brothers, Harry took on his first job as a paper delivery boy to help his mother run the household. His first official employment was in a large department store in Chicago, Field, Later and Company (which later became a part of Macy's), where he rose in the ranks and eventually became partner.

The department store made him wealthy. After a visit to England, he decided to settle in London and set up a store on its most prestigious shopping thoroughfare, Oxford Street. He named it after himself – Selfridge's – invested £400,000, and opened it to the public in 1909. Harry fully believed that shopping could be an enjoyable pursuit rather than a mere necessity. Selfridge's stood out from the competition due to its elaborate marketing campaigns, which perpetuated the idea that shopping was a premium leisure activity, a bold move in the years running up to World War One. Nevertheless, the store prospered.

Harry became a British citizen in 1937, but World War Two was his undoing: in 1941 the board of Selfridge's, heavily in debt, forced him out of the business. He survived for just six more years, dying at home in Putney of bronchial pneumonia. His legacy exists not only in his store, which continues to thrive today, but in his imaginative methods of making a department store a destination shop. He lived lavishly and his name retains its cachet.

Birthplace: Ripon, USA
Born: 1858 **Died:** 1947
Known for: Starting the department store Selfridge's

Henry Wellcome
Scientist

Pharmaceutical entrepreneur Henry Wellcome was born in
Wisconsin, USA, in 1853, to a family of missionaries. His father was
a reverend who enforced a strict religious upbringing. From a young
age, Henry worked in his uncle's pharmacy, sparking his interest in
pharmaceuticals.

When he was 27 years old, his friend Silas Burroughs, a travelling
pharmaceutical salesman, invited him to London, and together
they formed a company, Burroughs Wellcome & Co, which utilised
Henry's talent for combining pharmaceuticals with marketing. In
quick time, the company developed a medicine that could be used
in tablet form. This was trademarked as a 'tabloid,' and caught on in
part due to Henry's marketing nous: he would give out free samples
to doctors, which encouraged them not only to stock the tablets, but
also to prescribe them. In 1985, Silas died while on a cycling trip in
Monte Carlo, leaving Henry in control of Burroughs Wellcome & Co,
which later become the pharmaceutical giant GlaxoSmithKline.

In 1910, Henry became a British citizen and was knighted. He
died in 1936, and bequeathed a large portion of his wealth towards
improving human and animal health. The Wellcome Trust was
established in his name and remains one of the world's biggest
biomedical charities: it donates £900 million a year to scientific
projects. Henry's collection of 125,000 medical artefacts, including
Napoleon's toothbrush, are kept at the Wellcome Collection in
London, which attracts more than 700,000 visitors every year.

Birthplace: Wisconsin, USA
Born: 1853 **Died:** 1936
Known For: Founding
Burroughs Wellcome & Co,
now GlaxoSmithKline

Ida Copeland
Politician

Ida Fenzi, who became an influential advocate for the Girl Guides, was born in Tuscany, Italy in 1881 into a wealthy family with ties to Britain. Following her father's death, she moved to England with her mother, who married a London financier. In 1915, Ida herself married Ronald Copeland, chairman of the Spode-Copeland firm of bone china manufacturers in Staffordshire.

During World War One, Ida volunteered for the British Red Cross Society working in military hospitals. After the war, she continued her community work and became an active member of the Girl Guides, becoming one of its leading members and one of the reasons for its strong growth in Britain and worldwide. She continued her dedication to social causes by entering politics. In 1931, she ran to become a Conservative MP for Stoke-on-Trent against the fascist Sir Oswald Mosley. She won thanks to her dedication and empathy for local people, and became one of the first women to enter parliament.

She worked hard in the community, holding many positions, including Chairman of Stoke Division Women's Unionist Association and President of the Women's Advisory Council, Truro Division. As a refugee herself, she recognised the importance of helping individuals from abroad settle into British society and became Chairman of the Staffordshire Anglo Polish Society to further this work. Her rich and varied career helped swell the tide of sentiment that women should have a full role within politics and society.

Birthplace: Florence, Italy
Born: 1881 **Died:** 1964
Known For: Being one of the
first women to enter parliament

Ida Freund
Academic

Ida Freund was born in Austria in 1863 and brought up by her grandparents. Shortly after their deaths in 1881, she travelled to England to live under the care of her uncle Ludwig Straus, an eminent violinist. Despite speaking relatively little English, Ida won a place at Girton College, Cambridge, to study natural sciences. She graduated with first-class honours and a new-found passion for chemistry.

Having overcome the challenges faced by women who wanted to gain a higher education, Ida began working as a demonstrator at Newnham College and excelled in her work. In 1890, she became the first ever female chemistry lecturer in Britain. A champion of women's rights, she promoted a rounded scientific education for girls and campaigned for women to be admitted to the Chemical Society of London. She was remembered fondly by many of her students who were inspired and encouraged by her. She used imaginative techniques; she is credited with being the first to create 'periodic table cupcakes' to help students learn the elements, an idea adopted by other institutions.

She had almost finished writing her second chemistry textbook when she died following surgery in 1914. This work was later completed by her peers from Cambridge. Her two textbooks are still used in chemistry teaching today. Ida was posthumously honoured for her outstanding contribution to the natural sciences with the restoration of the chemistry lab at Newnham College in 1998 and the establishment of the Ida Freund Memorial Fund, which funds opportunities for further study for women who teach science.

Birthplace: Austria
Born: 1863 **Died:** 1914
Known For: Blazing a trail
for female university lecturers

Ira Aldridge
Actor and playwright

Ira Frederick Aldridge was born in July 1807 in New York City. His father, a preacher, hoped that his son would work for the church. But Ira was more interested in the theatre and attended the African-American run African Grove Theatre. He wanted to become an actor but felt that his prospects would be brighter in England where he hoped he would face less discrimination than in the United States. In 1824, he boarded a ship bound for Liverpool, and made his way across the Atlantic to a new life.

Ira made his British stage debut at the Royal Coburg Theatre in London the following year. He became the first African American to establish himself as an actor in another country. Nonetheless, he faced racial discrimination and his performances were often criticized for his supposed inexperience and poor speech. In London, he would often use his final address to convince the audience of the devastation and horror of slavery. After working in London, he played leading roles around the country, notably Shakespeare's Othello and Zanga in Edward Young's *The Revenge*. In his later career, he toured internationally, bringing Shakespeare's works to new audiences in Poland and Serbia.

He died in 1867 while on tour in Poland, aged 60, and is buried in Lodz. He is posthumously honoured around the globe, having received awards in Russia and Switzerland. His name is inscribed on a bronze plaque on the back of a seat in the stalls at the Shakespeare Memorial Theatre in Stratford-upon-Avon. A plaque at Coventry Theatre marks his tenure there as manager. The actor Adrian Lester starred as Ira in a play about his life, *Red Velvet*, in 2012.

Birthplace: New York, USA
Born: 1807 **Died:** 1867
Known For: Establishing a role
for black actors on the British stage

Iris Murdoch
Novelist

Iris Murdoch was born in Dublin, Ireland, to a well-off family in 1919. Her family moved her to London and she was sent to Badminton boarding school in Bristol. She received a first-class degree in classics, ancient history, and philosophy at the University of Oxford. After a brief spell at HM Treasury and various jobs working to aid refugees in camps across Europe, she studied philosophy as a postgraduate at the University of Cambridge and later taught the same subject at Oxford.

Her gift for language and her adventurous love life made her a skilled novelist. Her first works, *Under the Net* (1954) and *The Flight From The Enchanter* (1956), established her reputation as a writer adept at describing the intricacies of relationships. Her next novel, *The Bell* (1958), was a bestseller with 30,000 copies of the British edition printed within 10 weeks of publication. In all, she wrote 26 novels, along with a vast array of plays, poetry collections, essays and short stories. Her 19th novel *The Sea, the Sea,* won the Booker Prize in 1978.

In 1997, she was awarded the Golden PEN Award by English PEN for 'a Lifetime's Distinguished Service to Literature.' But by then her mental powers had been worn away by Alzheimer's disease and she died two years later in Oxford. Her struggle with dementia was captured in the film *Iris*, based on the memoirs of her husband John Bayley, a professor of English at the University of Oxford. In 2008, Iris was named by *The Times* as one of the 50 greatest British writers since 1945.

Birthplace: Dublin, Ireland
Born: 1919 **Died:** 1997
Known For: Writing
perceptive novels

Isaiah Berlin
Philosopher

Isaiah Berlin was born in Riga, Latvia (then part of the Russian empire) in 1909 to a wealthy Jewish family. After the October revolution in 1917, his family left Russia, fleeing anti-Semitism and Bolshevik oppression. They arrived in Britain when Isaiah was just 11. Isaiah could barely speak a word of English, but within a year he was fluent; an early indicator of his vast intelligence.

Isaiah attended various schools in London before being admitted to the University of Oxford to study classics, graduating with first-class honours. He took a second degree in philosophy, politics and economics and, aged 23, was elected to a prize fellowship at All Souls College. He was barred from entering the British army during World War Two because of his Latvian roots, and instead worked for the British Diplomatic Service in the United States, relaying intelligence to London. On returning to Oxford, he became Chichele Professor of Social and Political Theory from 1957 to 1967. His greatest contribution to philosophy during a dazzling career was acknowledging the importance to an individual of a sense of belonging, which could take many forms, as it had during his life.

Since his death in 1997, Isaiah's life, dedicated to the pursuit of knowledge, has been memorialized in Oxford with buildings and a scholarship established in his name by Oxford University. In 2011, the Isaiah Berlin Association of Latvia was founded to support the ideas and values expressed and defended by him of 'pluralism, tolerance and individual liberty.'

Birthplace: Riga, Latvia
Born: 1909 **Died:** 1997
Known For: Revitalising
liberal thought

Jacob Epstein
Sculptor

———————————

Jacob Epstein was born in New York City to a Polish-Jewish family. As a child, he spent long periods of time ill with pleurisy and believed that the time he spent alone drawing was the reason for his later success as an artist. He began sculpting while at night school. In 1902, he moved to Paris to study, and three years later arrived in London where he moved in bohemian circles. His early, rough-hewn sculptures gained notoriety for shunning Roman and Greek classicism in favour of bolder influences from West Africa, India and Pacific islands. Some of his early nudes were too explicit for Edwardian sensibilities and were damaged or covered up by amateur censors.

In 1914, Jacob became connected with the Vorticism movement that expressed the dynamism of the modern world through sharp angles and bold lines. He sculpted several notable figures of the time, among them Arsenal's title-winning manager Herbert Chapman, the Welsh Poet WH Davies, and the heads of the Navy, Army and Air Force, respectively Sir Andrew Cunningham, Sir Alan Cunningham, and Sir Charles Portal. He also rendered leading British politicians of the 1940s, including the Foreign Secretary Ernest Bevin, Chancellor of the Exchequer John Anderson, and Winston Churchill.

Jacob was knighted in 1954. His art continues to be on display in major galleries including the National Portrait Gallery and Tate Britain in London and the Pompidou Centre in Paris. He died in London on 19 August 1959, and was buried at Putney Vale Cemetery. His statues can be seen all over England and Wales, from Parliament Square to Liverpool.

———————————

Birthplace: New York, USA
Born: 1880 **Died:** 1959
Known For: Pioneering
modern sculpture

Jimi Hendrix
Musician

'Jimi', born James Marshall Hendrix, in 1942 in Seattle, Washington, had a volatile childhood and sought solace in music. Long before he could afford to buy a guitar, he would emulate playing one with a wooden broom. His first musical instrument was a banjo with one string, which he learned to play by ear. (Later, he would famously play guitar with his teeth.) He was playing acoustic guitar, and forming his first band, by the age of 15, but regularly got in trouble with the law. Eventually, the police who gave him an ultimatum: join the army, or go to prison. He chose the former but a life in uniform was never going to satisfy a free spirit for very long, and he left in order to pursue music full-time.

Throughout the early 1960s, Jimi toured the United States with limited success: Americans were not entirely sure how to take him. In 1966, he approached the *Rolling Stones'* manager Andrew Loog Oldham in the hope that Oldham might manage him, but was summarily turned down. He moved to London, where he quickly signed a contract with ex-*Animals* manager Michael Jeffery. Here, he formed the Jimi Hendrix Experience. They had three UK top 10 hits in quick succession: *Hey Joe, Purple Haze* and *The Wind Cries Mary*. America started to take note, and by 1968 his album *Electric Ladyland* reached number one in the Billboard charts.

Jimi's style, often imitated but never matched, revelled in the sound of the feedback between the guitar and the amplifier, and it was in pursuit of this that he often lost himself, occasionally playing his cherished instrument with his teeth, and even once setting it on fire. He died in 1970, from drugs, at what would become a fabled age for troubled rock stars: 27.

Birthplace: Seattle, USA
Born: 1942 **Died:** 1970
Known For: Dazzling audiences
with his guitar playing

Joan Armatrading
Musician

Grammy-nominated singer-songwriter Joan Armatrading was born on the island of St Kitts in 1950, the third of six children. When she was three, her parents left the Caribbean for the UK with her two older siblings, and settled in a district of Birmingham. Joan herself was sent to Antigua to live her grandmother. She was subsequently brought over to the UK at the age of seven. By her mid-teens, she was gravitating towards music, perhaps in part influenced by her father who used to play in a band, though her father always forbade his children from touching his guitar.

She signed her first recording contract in the early 1970s, and released her debut album, *Whatever's for Us*, in 1972. The BBC DJ John Peel was an early fan. By 1976, she was among the most celebrated singers in the country, her self-titled album a big hit that spawned the timeless hit ballad, *Love and Affection*. In an era where singers of colour tended to be compartmentalised – into reggae, or soul, or blues, or jazz – Joan was a pop star whose appeal was as broad as it was international. Many of her singles would go on to attain classic status, the likes of *Drop the Pilot*, *Down to Zero* and *Me Myself and I* still staples of UK radio play today. In 1996, she was awarded an Ivor Novello Award for her Outstanding Song Collection, and also received a Lifetime Achievement Award from the BBC, which named her one of the 100 Most Influential Women in Rock Music.

Outside of music, Joan served as the President of the Women of the Year Lunches for five years, and in 2001 was made an OBE. She has inspired a generation of songwriters across the world, and continues to release albums and tour widely.

Birthplace: Basseterre, St Kitts
Born: 1950
Known For: Writing heartfelt songs including *Love and Affection*

Johanna Weber
Engineer

Johanna Weber was born in Düsseldorf, Germany into a poor farming family. At the age of four her father died in World War One, qualifying her to receive financial support for her education. She studied chemistry and mathematics and she graduated from the University of Göttingen with a first-class degree in 1935. She went into teacher training. However, she could not become a teacher because she was not a member of the Nazi Party so instead found work close to her mother and sister in an armaments company called Krupp. In 1939, Johanna took up a position at the Aerodynamics Research Institute in Göttingen where she met a life-long friend, Dietrich Küchemann.

In 1945, Göttingen was captured by the US Army and fell into the British occupation zone. One year later, along with Dietrich, she joined the aerodynamics department at the Royal Aircraft Establishment in Farnborough. She improved the design of the wings and airflow of the Handley Page Victor bomber. She also worked on the calculations for the wings of the Vickers VC10 airliner and without her the Airbus A300B may never have been commercially successfully. In response to Johanna and Dietrich's research into supersonic transport, in 1956 the new Supersonic Transport Advisory Committee put their work into action, culminating in the construction of Concorde, the Anglo-French supersonic airliner.

Johanna wrote approximately 100 scientific papers by the time she retired in 1975. She spent the remainder of her life living in Surrey and took geology and psychology courses at the University of Surrey, prior to her death in 2014, aged 104.

Birthplace: Düsseldorf, Germany
Born: 1910 **Died:** 2014
Known For: Contributing to the development of the Airbus A300B

John Barnes
Footballer

John Barnes was born in Kingston, Jamaica. His father was an officer in the Jamaica Defence Force and was in the Jamaican football team in the 1950s. John was encouraged to play football from an early age and when the family moved to London in 1976, he began playing for Stowe Boys Club in Paddington. His ability was quickly spotted and, in 1981, he signed for Watford, making his debut that year.

After six years at Watford, he moved to Liverpool, where he thrived under manager Kenny Dalglish. At Liverpool, John made 407 appearances, scored 108 goals and filled his trophy cabinet with two league titles, two FA Cup winner's medals, two runner's up medals, and a League Cup winner's medal. He encountered racism (people would throw bananas onto the pitch) during his long career, which was also darkened by the Hillsborough disaster, which claimed the lives of 96 Liverpool fans. John attended several of their funerals and visited the injured in hospital. After 10 years at Anfield he moved to Newcastle.

In 1983, he made his debut for England under Sir Bobby Robson and became one of the first black players to claim to claim a regular place in the national side. A year later, he scored a 'miracle' goal against Brazil in the Maracana, dribbling past five players before slotting the ball coolly into the net. He went on to score 11 goals in 79 appearances, playing alongside other England greats such as Gary Lineker, Peter Beardsley and Chris Waddle. In 2005, he was inducted into the English Football Hall of Fame.

Birthplace: Jamaica
Born: 1963
Known For: Being a key member
of one of the best football teams

John Edmonstone
Naturalist

John Edmonstone's origins are the subject of speculation, but historians believe that he was born into slavery in present-day Guyana, South America, during the late 18th Century. While a slave, he is thought to have been taught the art of taxidermy by the family of his master, the naturalist Charles Waterton, with whom he would catch exotic birds to preserve and study.

In 1807, John was brought to Scotland, where he was later freed and began to teach taxidermy skills at the University of Edinburgh. He lived on Lothian Street, a few doors down from the biologist and explorer Charles Darwin, who started studying medicine at the university in 1825. Darwin became disillusioned and instead took taxidermy lessons with John. They became good friends and, during the long hours they spent together, John would tell Darwin tales of his homeland, describing rainforests filled with animals and plants unseen by Europeans and landscapes wildly different from Scotland's hills. Many suggest that the rich imagery he painted ignited Darwin's desire to explore unknown lands and their flora and fauna. Soon after, Darwin enrolled as an on-board naturalist on the *HMS Beagle*'s historic round-the-world voyage. John's lessons proved invaluable to Darwin, whose taxidermy specimens allowed him to theorize on evolution.

John may also have told Darwin of the horrors of slavery, encouraging his friend to disregard the prejudiced assumptions about race of the time and instead look to more scientifically based theories of human and animal origins. The latter half of John's life remains a mystery, but in 2009 his contribution to scientific knowledge was fixed in the public consciousness when a plaque was placed by his old home on Lothian Street.

Birthplace: Guyana, South America
Born: 1793 **Died:** 1822
Known For: Teaching taxidermy to Charles Darwin

Joseph Conrad
Author

Often regarded as one of the finest novelists to write in the English language, Joseph Conrad didn't actually speak fluent English until he reached his mid-20s. Born in Berdychiv, Ukraine in 1857, which was then part of the Russian Empire, he grew up in a country that was actively trying to establish independence, and with a writer and political activist father who did his best to document the nation's efforts. As a direct result, the family were forced to move frequently.

His father proved an earnest teacher, and fed the young Joseph a diet of Shakespeare and Victor Hugo, whose influence would later dominate his own writing. Joseph's mother died in 1865 of tuberculosis, his father following four years later, claimed by the same illness, orphaning their only son at the age of 11. Perhaps fuelled by his early readings of Hugo's *Toilers of the Sea*, Joseph moved to Marseille in 1874 to work as a merchant, first on French ships, then British ones. He did this for the next 15 years, and his life at sea would serve as inspiration for his later life as a master of English literature. Many of his characters stem from his nautical career and the people he met while travelling around the world.

Though he was largely nomadic, constantly on the move, he frequently returned to Britain, and became a British citizen in 1886, where he remained until he died at home in Kent in 1924. Averse to public recognition, he once turned down the offer of a British knighthood, but his books – which include *The Secret Agent* and *Heart of Darkness* – live on, and have been cited as influencing the writing of, among others, TS Eliot, F Scott Fitzgerald and George Orwell.

Birthplace: Berdychiv, Ukraine
Born: 1857 **Died:** 1924
Known For: Writing
Heart of Darkness

Joseph Rotblat
Physicist

Joseph Rotblat was born in Warsaw to Polish-Jewish parents, whose business collapsed during World War One and could not afford to send him into further education. Joseph worked hard to fulfill his dream of becoming a physicist. He eventually graduated from the Free University of Poland and then Warsaw University, becoming a Doctor of Physics in 1938. His study of particle physics made him realise that a nuclear reaction could release vast energy.

He was invited to study in Britain under Sir James Chadwick, who discovered the neutron. During World War Two, Joseph was part of the research team working on Tube Alloys, the codename of the British team researching nuclear weapons. At the time, he believed that the Allies needed to develop a nuclear bomb to prevent Nazi Germany from using one. Following a brief stint in America assisting The Manhattan Project, the US research into nuclear weapons, where his reservations about atomic bombs grew, he accepted a position as a senior lecturer at the University of Liverpool.

After atomic bombs were dropped on Japan, Joseph became increasingly opposed to the use of nuclear weapons and conducted research on the devastating effects of fallout on living organisms. His work contributed to the 1957 Partial Test Ban Treaty which ended atmospheric testing. In 1994, he shared the Nobel Peace Prize 'for efforts to diminish the part played by nuclear arms in international affairs and, in the longer run, to eliminate such arms.'

Birthplace: Warsaw, Poland
Born: 1908 **Died:** 2005
Known For: Limiting the
spread of nuclear weapons

Judith Kerr
Author

The woman who would go on to become one of the best loved children's authors of all time was born in Berlin in 1923. Her father, Alfred Kerr, a theatre critic, was an outspoken critic of the Nazis and, in 1933, the Kerrs were forced to flee Germany. They ended up briefly in Switzerland, then France, before settling in Britain. Judith never forgot having to leave behind all their possessions, including a beloved pink rabbit comforter that would inspire a later book.

During World War Two, Judith worked for the Red Cross and won a scholarship to the Central School of Arts and Crafts. She became an artist and later worked as a scriptwriter for the BBC, but she achieved worldwide renown for her books, which she wrote and illustrated herself. The Thomas family, who feature in her popular Mog series of books about a friendly cat, were based on her husband's family name 'Thomas', while the names of the two children – Matthew and Tacy – are her own children's middle names.

Judith would also write a trilogy of semi-autobiographical novels based on her early life experiences. *Out Of the Hitler Time* comprised three books: *When Hitler Stole Pink Rabbit, Bombs on Aunty Dainty* and *A Small Person Far Away*. Each has since been used in British and German schools to introduce children to the realities of World War Two. Judith is most celebrated for her classic *The Tiger Who Came to Tea*. First published in 1968, it is one of the bestselling children's books of all time. In 2013, the UK's first bilingual German and British school in south London was named after her. She wrote until she died in 2019, aged 95.

Birthplace: Berlin, Germany
Born: 1923 **Died:** 2019
Known For: Writing
The Tiger Who Came to Tea

Karan Bilimoria
Entrepreneur

Karan Bilimoria was born in 1961 in Hyderabad, India, into a family of Zoroastrian Parsi descent. His father and grandfather were high-ranking officers in the Indian army. After attending school and university in India, Karan studied accounting at London Metropolitan University and qualified as a chartered accountant with what is today Ernst & Young. While taking a law degree at the University of Cambridge, he joined the polo team. He noticed that the polo sticks he played with in India were higher quality than those at Cambridge, so he began importing and selling them profitably to the department store Harrods and Lillywhites, a sports outfitters. This was the start of his business career.

Karan adored Indian cuisine but felt that the British beer served alongside it was too gassy and ruined enjoyment of the meal. He and his friend, Arjun Reddy, came up with the idea of producing a beer that would better complement the food. In 1989, they founded Cobra Beer. They began brewing the beer in India and importing it to Britain. With the rising popularity of curry houses in Britain, sales rocketed to £1 million in five years. By 2001, they had hit £13 million and Cobra was bought by Molson Coors, a multinational brewing group.

In 2005, Karan helped to establish the Cobra Foundation to provide health, education and community support for young people in South Asia, particularly by providing safe water. In 2006, he became an independent crossbench life peer in the House of Lords. In 2014, he was made Chancellor of the University of Birmingham.

Birthplace: Hyderabad, India
Born: 1961
Known For: Launching
Cobra Beer

Karel Kuttelwascher
Fighter pilot

Karel Kuttelwascher was born in 1916 in what is now the Czech Republic, to parents of German origin. He gave up a job as a clerk at a flour mill to train as a fighter pilot in the Czechoslovakian Air Force. When Germany occupied Czechoslovakia in 1939, he fled the country, aged 18, hiding in a coal train. He made his way first to Poland, then to France, where he and his colleagues joined the French Air Force to continue the fight against the Germans. While in France, Karel shot down at least two Luftwaffe planes. In 1940 when France surrendered, he flew to Algeria, took a train to Morocco, boarded a boat to Gibraltar, and sailed for Britain.

He joined the Royal Air Force and was assigned to No 1 Squadron, its oldest unit. He quickly made a name for himself in the cockpit of a Hawker Hurricane during the Battle of Britain and, later, during the Channel Dash, an operation to sink German destroyers. In 1942, he joined night intruder operations to destroy German planes as they returned to their own airfields. These missions were conducted during a full moon without radar, and required supreme piloting skill and bravery. Karel downed the most aircraft of any night intruder, earning him the Distinguished Flying Cross and the nickname 'Night Reaper.'

In all, he shot down 18 German aircraft, one of dozens of Czech and Polish airmen to help the Allied air war. He returned to Czechoslovakia in peacetime only to return to Britain a year later because of the rise of the Communist Party. In 1956, he became a naturalised British subject. He died three years later of a heart attack, aged 42.

Birthplace: Czechoslovakia
Born: 1916 **Died:** 1959
Known For: Protecting Britain
during World War Two

Krystyna Skarbek
Wartime spy

Christine Glanville was reputedly Winston Churchill's favourite spy and inspired the character Vesper Lynd in Ian Fleming's first James Bond book, *Casino Royale*. Her real name, though, was Krystyna Skarbek. She was born in 1908 in Warsaw, Poland, into a fading, part-Jewish aristocratic family. When it fell on hard times in the 1920s, she was forced to take an office job at a car dealership. The exhaust fumes from the garage below permanently damaged her lungs – and made her reluctant to do admin work again.

When Germany invaded Poland in 1939, she sought out a very different line of work. She took a boat to Britain, travelled to London and suggested to the Secret Intelligence Service that she become a spy. MI6 agreed – and approved a dangerous first mission from Hungary. With the aid of a friend in the Polish Olympic ski team, Krystyna skied across the wintry Tatra mountains into Poland laden with propaganda documents. In Warsaw, she met Polish resistance leaders and reported intelligence back to London. She embarked on further operations in occupied Europe, including an occasion when she identified herself as a British agent and threatened, charmed, harangued and bribed a Gestapo commander into freeing two colleagues from a French prison hours before they were due to be executed. Resourceful, determined and fearless, she enjoyed an exceptional reputation in the British intelligence community.

After the war, she received the George Medal and the Croix de Guerre. In 1952, she was murdered by a spurned suitor. Details of her wartime activities were kept secret for decades, but the truth slowly emerged. In 2017, a bronze bust of Krystyna was unveiled at the Polish Hearth Club in London.

Birthplace: Trzepnica, Poland
Born: 1908 **Died:** 1952
Known For: Undertaking missions behind enemy lines

Kylie Minogue
Pop singer

Kylie Minogue, who would go on to become famous first as a car mechanic in a daytime soap opera then as a popstar, was born in Melbourne, Australia, in 1968. A child actress, she appeared in several popular soap operas, before landing the role as Charlene on *Neighbours*, which became the most-watched soap in the UK in the early 1990s.

Alongside Jason Donovan, who played her on-screen boyfriend before also becoming her off-screen boyfriend, Kylie captivated Australia and Britain, too. After reaching number one with her debut single *I Should Be So Lucky*, she moved to the UK, where she promptly became a chart regular, her hits including *The Locomotion, Better the Devil You Know, Spinning Around* and *Can't Get You Out Of My Head*, another number one, and which sold over a million copies in Britain and five million worldwide.

She has been one of our more enduring pop stars ever since. She has won a Grammy and three Brit Awards, and is these days seen as a British national treasure. She campaigns for charities including ChildLine and the National Society for the Prevention of Cruelty to Children. In 2017, she was recognised by the Britain-Australia society for helping to improve the relationship between the UK and Australia. She was appointed an OBE for services to music in 2008. Her Legends slot at Glastonbury 2019 was the most-watched Glastonbury performance ever, seen by 3.2 million people.

Birthplace: Melbourne, Australia
Born: 1968
Known For: Singing
bubbly pop songs

Lew Grade
Broadcaster

The future cigar-chomping media tycoon Lew Grade was born Louis Winogradsky in 1906, into a Jewish family in Tokmak in the Russian Empire near the Black Sea. As with so many other Jewish families of the era, the Winogradskys were forced to flee anti-Semitism and spiralling Cossack violence, and ended up in Brick Lane in London.

By 15, Lew had followed his father into the clothing industry, but an abiding love for dancing would lead him away from the rag trade. In 1926, he won the World Cup Charleston Championships at the Royal Albert Hall. He was now a professional dancer on an impressive £50 a week. But he soon realised that he might make more of his life if he became a talent scout. He quit dancing, and set up an agency with Joe Collins, father of Jackie and Joan, and later moved to the United States.

While in North America, Lew expanded his client list, and started to represent some of the biggest names in entertainment, among them Louis Armstrong. In the 1950s, he became involved with a small TV production company called Associated Television. He later took control of the company, which made such hit series as *The Adventures of Robin Hood, Crossroads,* and *Bullseye.* He also produced a number of popular kids shows, including *Captain Scarlet* and *Thunderbirds,* and was instrumental in bringing *The Muppet Show,* one of the biggest shows in America, to British screens in 1976. He went on to work as a producer for Andrew Lloyd Webber's *Starlight Express,* while occupying various other high-profile positions within the entertainment industry. He was knighted in 1969 and made a life peer in 1976, becoming Lord Grade of Elstree.

Birthplace: Tokmak, Ukraine
Born: 1906 **Died:** 1998
Known For: Bringing
Thunderbirds and *The Muppet
Show* to UK televisions

Lucian Freud
Painter

Lucian Freud was born in Berlin in 1922, the grandson of the renowned psychiatrist Sigmund Freud and the son of the architect Ernst Freud. His family fled Nazi Germany in the early 1930s and settled in St John's Wood, London. He attended the Central School of Art in London and briefly served in the Navy during World War Two, before returning to his studies at Goldsmith College, graduating in 1943.

He began his career as an illustrator and painter, favouring a surrealist style that depicted animals and people. His reputation grew quickly and he held his first solo exhibition, at London's Lefevre Gallery, in 1944. As his work developed, so too did his style, his focus shifting towards portraiture and figurative works. He would often spend hours with those he painted, in pursuit not only of building up a rapport, but also understanding them better in the interest of the piece. His work soon became distinctive, particularly his nudes, which constituted the majority of his work over a 50 year period.

During his later career, he became a lead figure in a collective of artists named The School of London, a movement focused on figurative drawing. Its members included the prominent artist Francis Bacon, previously a model of Lucien's. Several of his paintings have sold for tens of millions of pounds, and in 2008 his piece *Benefits Supervisor Resting* sold for $33.6 million, which at the time was the highest price paid for a work by living artist. He spent much of his life living in London, in a house with a studio in Kensington. He died in 2011 at the age of 88. He is buried in Highgate Cemetery.

Birthplace: Berlin, Germany
Born: 1922 **Died:** 2011
Known For: Painting some of the
20th Century's greatest portraits

Ludwig Goldscheider
Publisher

Ludwig Goldscheider was born in Vienna, Austria in 1896. After World War One, he studied art history at the University of Vienna, where he was taught by a distinguished art historian, Julius von Schlosser. In 1923, Ludwig co-founded a publishing company, Phaidon, with two colleagues to promote their passion for the classical world and its culture (Phaidon being a pupil of Plato). During the 1930s, the company published books of high art at a low price.

After the Nazis marched into Vienna, Ludwig moved to Britain. In London, he and his colleague Béla Horovitz re-opened Phaidon Press. They managed the company together until Béla's sudden death in 1955. In 1950, Phaidon Press published *The Story of Art* by Sir Ernst Gombrich (*featured on page 73*), a work tracing the evolution of art from primitive times to the modern era. It became the bestselling art book of all time, selling over seven million copies in multiple languages.

Ludwig was also the author, editor, and designer of several other studies, including of Leonardo da Vinci and Michelangelo. Scholars around the world recognised his wide knowledge of art. In 1973, he marked Phaidon's golden jubilee: 50 years of making excellent books. He died a few months later. From its headquarters in London and New York, Phaidon Press has more than 1,500 titles in print, is renowned for its beautiful illustrated titles, and has sold 42 million books worldwide.

Birthplace: Vienna, Austria
Born: 1896 **Died:** 1973
Known For: Founding the world-renowned Phaidon Press

Ludwig Guttmann
Neurologist

Ludwig Guttman (affectionately known as 'Poppa') was born in July 1899 in Prussia to Jewish parents. He developed an interest in medicine and the anatomy in 1917 while doing voluntary work at a hospital specialising in accidents and injuries. He studied medicine at the University of Breslau, graduating in 1924. By 1933, he was an accomplished neurosurgeon. With the rise of Nazism, he was restricted to working at the Jewish Hospital in Breslau, whose director he became. He encouraged his staff to admit as many patients as possible during the 'Kristallnacht' attacks on Jewish people and prevented 60 of his 64 patients from being deported to concentration camps.

He escaped to England in 1939 with the aid of the Council for Assisting Refugee Academics and settled in Oxford with his wife and two children. At the request of the government, in 1944, he established a national spinal injuries unit at Stoke Mandeville Hospital. He felt strongly that sports and physical fitness were crucial for building strength and confidence, especially for injured military veterans. He organised a sporting event specifically for disabled people to take place on the same day as the Olympic Games. The inaugural Stoke Mandeville Games were held on 29 July 1948.

Over the years, the Stoke Mandeville Games attracted an increasing number of competitors and spectators. Four years after Ludwig's death from a heart attack in 1980, the games were renamed the Paralympics (with para meaning 'beside'), aligning them with the Olympics. Athletes from 159 countries competed in 22 events at the 2016 Rio Paralympics, watched by an estimated worldwide TV audience of 4.1 billion.

Birthplace: Toszek, Poland
Born: 1899 **Died:** 1980
Known For: Establishing the
Paralympic Games

Magdi Yacoub
Heart surgeon

The famous heart transplant surgeon Magdi Yacoub was born in 1935 in Bilbeis, Egypt. From an early age he wanted to follow his father's footsteps into the operating theatre. When his aunt died of heart complications, he decided to specialise in cardiac medicine. He studied at Cairo University, becoming a doctor in 1957. He taught at the University of Chicago, before moving to Britain, where he became a consultant cardiothoracic surgeon at Harefield Hospital in London.

Magdi performed the UK's first successful heart and lung surgery at Harefield. His team carried out more than 1,000 heart and lung transplants, saving the lives of hundreds of people, including high-profile individuals such as the comedian Eric Morecambe and the actor Omar Sharif. In 1988, he performed an open-heart triple bypass surgery on the Greek Prime Minister Andreas Papandreou, who credited him with saving his life. In 2013, a patient he operated on in 1982, John McCafferty, entered the Guinness Book of World Records for being the world's longest-surviving heart transplant patient.

Magdi was appointed professor at the National Heart and Lung Institute in 1986, where he continued to develop more sophisticated techniques for transplanting hearts and lungs. He also pioneered a technique for combating a congenital heart defect in babies. He led a team that grew part of a human heart valves from stem cells for the first time. As well as his contribution to advancing surgical techniques in Britain, he has assisted healthcare programmes in Egypt, Mozambique, Ethiopia and Jamaica. In 2001, he retired from performing surgery for the NHS but continues to work with his charity Chain of Hope.

Birthplace: Bilbeis, Egypt
Born: 1935
Known For: Carrying out the first
successful heart and lung surgery

Malala Yousafzai
Campaigner

Malala Yousafzai was born in Swat District, Pakistan, in 1992 to a Sunni Muslim family. Her father was an educational activist who inspired his daughter to take an interest in politics and educational rights for women. In 2007, the Taliban took control and quickly enforced strict Islamic laws that banned girls from going to school, shopping, watching television, or dancing. Malala was determined to continue with her education, and began writing for the BBC about her desire to attend school. She gave interviews to journalists about her life in such a restricted part of the world.

In 2011, aged 14, she was nominated for the International Children's Peace Prize by Archbishop Desmond Tutu, and two months later won Pakistan's inaugural National Youth Peace Prize. Her public profile was increasing, and she was becoming something of an icon. She was frequently praised for her bravery. In 2012, as she was riding home from school, Malala was shot in the head by a Taliban gunman. She survived the attack but was in such a critical condition that she was transferred overseas, to Queen Elizabeth Hospital in Birmingham, where she was operated on. In 2013, she was finally discharged.

Her family remained in the Midlands and Malala has continued to live in Britain, promoting education for young women across the world through her charitable organisation, the Malala Fund. In 2014, she was the co-recipient of the Nobel Peace Prize for her devotion to fighting for the right of all children to an education, calling on world leaders to invest in 'books, not bullets.' At 17, she was the youngest ever Nobel Laureate. In 2013, she published her memoir, *I Am Malala*.

Birthplace: Swat District, Pakistan
Born: 1992
Known For: Campaigning
for girls' education

Marc Isambard Brunel
Engineer

Marc Isambard Brunel was born in 1769 in Normandy, France to a prosperous farming family. From a young age, he was enthralled by design and craftsmanship and was often found drawing and making objects. His first job was a cabinetmaker. But when the French Revolution began in 1789, he was a naval cadet in the West Indies. He was a Royalist sympathiser and, on his return to France, left for the United States. Whilst there, he returned to his childhood ambitions and became chief engineer of New York in 1796. He continued to hone his professional skills, before moving to Britain in 1799.

Marc worked on big infrastructure projects, mainly in London. One of his most notable achievements was the development of a method for moving pulleys mechanically rather than by manual labour, an innovation that was used in shipbuilding. He also invented and patented the tunnelling shield, a device that allowed unstable ground to be excavated. He used it to dig the first tunnel under the River Thames. In its first 15 weeks of opening, the tunnel was used by one million people, including Queen Victoria and Prince Albert. The passage later became part of the London Underground and still exists as the East London line, which carries thousands of passengers across London every day.

In 1841, Marc was knighted by Queen Victoria but his hard work left him in ill health and he died at the age of 80 in 1849. His engineering legacy was furthered by his son, Isambard Kingdom Brunel, who built steamships and the Great Western Railway and, in 2002, was voted the second greatest Briton, after Winston Churchill.

Birthplace: Normandy, France
Born: 1769 **Died:** 1849
Known For: Building
the Thames Tunnel

Margaret Busby
Journalist and publisher

Margaret Busby, a Ghanaian-born writer and publisher, was born in Accra, Gold Coast, in 1944, to a family with strong links to prominent journalists, politicians and authors. She moved to Britain and went to school in Sussex. She left school at 15, but later went to London University. With her friend Clive Allison in 1967, she set up the publishing company Allison & Busby, making her Britain's first black female publisher.

Allison & Busby aimed to give young people access to affordable books, which were sold on the streets for just five shillings. Although the firm didn't work exclusively with black authors, it was instrumental in telling the black British experience through literature. Among others, it published Sam Greenlee's *The Spook Who Sat by the Door*, Buchi Emecheta's *Second-Class Citizens* and CLR James' *The Black Jacobins*.

Margaret left the company 1987 to focus on writing and activism. Her most celebrated work was *Daughters of Africa* in 1992, a compilation of 200 pieces of literature from women across the African diaspora. It is considered a pioneering work and inspired the Margaret Busby New Daughters of Africa Award which honours the achievements of female African students. She co-authored a number of other works including *Colours of a New Day: Writing for South Africa* and *Carnival: A Photographic and Testimonial History of the Notting Hill Carnival*. In 2017, she was elected an honorary fellow of the Royal Society of Literature and awarded the Benson Medal for lifelong achievement.

Birthplace: Accra, Ghana
Born: 1944
Known For: Being Britain's first
black female book publisher

Marie Tussaud
Entrepreneur

By the time Marie Tussaud was born in 1761 in Strasbourg, France, her father had been killed in the Seven Years' War . Her mother moved their family to Switzerland to live with a Swiss physician, Philippe Curtius, who used wax modelling to portray anatomy. Philippe realised that he could turn this craft into an art-form and began modelling portraits of prominent figures. His skill and precision became widely recognised and he trained Marie. She developed a talent for modelling, and created wax figures of notable individuals such as the French writer Voltaire.

During the French Revolution, Marie's royalist connections were taken for sympathies. She was arrested and prepared for death by the guillotine but was pardoned by a good friend. In return however, she was forced to pay for her freedom in a grisly manner: by making death masks of guillotined royalists. Among others, she modeled Louis XVI, Marie Antoinette and Robespierre. In 1802, she travelled to London with her two sons, a collection of her wax works and the inherited models of her old teacher Philippe, who had died by the guillotine eight years earlier. She travelled across Britain with her exhibition until she found it a permanent home in Baker Street, London. After Marie's death 1850, her family continued collecting wax figures for display. Despite a large fire in 1925 and German bombing in 1941, her museum still stands on the site.

Now named Madame Tussauds, it is one of London's most popular attractions. Hundreds of monarchs, prime ministers, actors, pop stars and other notable individuals are rendered in life-size models for the entertainment and education of visitors. Marie Tussaud herself looks out into the crowds at Madame Tussauds in Orlando, one of 24 Madam Tussauds around the world.

Birthplace: Strasbourg, France
Born: 1761 **Died:** 1850
Known For: Founding
Madame Tussauds waxworks

Mary Prince
Campaigner

Mary Prince was born in 1788 in Bermuda to an enslaved family of African descent. She was sold to an owner in the Turks and Caicos Islands, who made her toil in the salt ponds, where she suffered from exposure. As a young woman, she was sold again to the Wood family in Antigua where she was kept as a household slave. During her time in Antigua, Mary joined the Moravian Church, learned how to read and met a former slave, Daniel James, whom she married in 1826. Her master, John Adams Wood, detested the presence of a free former slave and frequently flogged Marie.

She accompanied the Wood family to England in 1828, but was unable to return to Antigua by new laws banning the transportation of slaves from England. Instead, she escaped from the Woods and met Thomas Pringle, an anti-slavery campaigner who offered her help and encouraged her to appeal to the government to gain her freedom. She became the first woman ever to present a petition to parliament: it was rejected. Instead, in 1831, she and Pringle published *The History of Mary Prince*, making her the first black woman, and first enslaved woman, to publish an autobiography. The book exposed the horrors endured by slaves in the West Indies, and stoked the growing anti-slavery sentiment in England.

After the events detailed in her book, little is known of Mary's fate. She may have remained in England for the rest of her life, although some speculate that she returned to the West Indies as a free woman following the 1834 Slavery Abolition Act. Her extraordinary life is commemorated in a display at the Museum in Docklands and by a plaque near her home in Bloomsbury, London. No confirmed photographs or images of her face exist.

Birthplace: Bermuda
Born: 1788 **Died:** 1833
Known For: Revealing the
horrors of slavery

Mary Seacole
Nurse

Mary Seacole was born in 1805 in Kingston, Jamaica to a Jamaican mother and a Scottish father. Her mother was skilled in traditional medicine which Mary adopted from an early age, experimenting on pets before her mother allowed her to help treat people. Her father was a lieutenant in the British Army, which exposed her to the practices of military doctors.

She visited London in 1821 but did not stay for long. She spent much of her life travelling between Caribbean islands expanding her knowledge of medicine. In 1854, she returned to London to volunteer as a nurse to treat British soldiers in the Crimean War. She was repeatedly turned down, so she made her way to Turkey under her own steam. On her arrival she used spare pieces of local material to build the 'British Hotel,' which provided 'a mess-table and comfortable quarters for sick and convalescent officers.' Mary also tended to the wounded on the battlefield. After the war she returned to England ill and financially destitute – a struggle highlighted by the press. The Prince of Wales, the Duke of Edinburgh and the Duke of Cambridge contributed to a fund that helped her out of bankruptcy. She remained in London until her death in 1881.

Mary is commemorated by many British buildings and monuments, including the Mary Seacole Centre for Nursing Practice at Thames Valley University. A blue plaque marks her previous home at 14 Soho Square in central London. In 2004, she was voted the greatest black Briton in a BBC poll.

Birthplace: Kingston, Jamaica
Born: 1805 **Died:** 1881
Known For: Caring for wounded soldiers in the Crimean War

Maureen Dunlop de Popp
Pilot

Maureen Adele Chase Dunlop de Popp was born in Buenos Aires in 1920, to an Australian father and English mother. The Dunlop family regularly visited England, where Maureen took flying lessons. She decided to become a pilot. After forging her date of birth to make herself appear older, she took further flying training in Buenos Aires, spending many hours perfecting her skills.

At the outbreak of World War Two, she wanted to fight against the Nazis and, in 1942, left South America on a boat for England. Having dedicated much of her time to gaining the solo flying hours a woman needed to join the British Air Transport Auxiliary – double those demanded of a man – Maureen enrolled as one of its few female pilots. ATA pilots delivered aircraft to soldiers on the front line and would only find out what type of aeroplane they were flying on the day of the job. She had to be able to pilot the many different types of aircraft used during the war, including Spitfires and Wellington Bombers.

Maureen was part of an all-female ATA squadron that delivered new Spitfires. When officials recognised that the work they were carrying out was just as good as that of the men, she and her female colleagues received equal pay. However, much to her dismay, female pilots were deemed unable to fly in combat. She spent three years in the ATA. Following the war, she continued to fly, joining the RAF and later becoming a commercial pilot, before settling in Norwich to raise her family. She died in Norfolk in 2012 at the age of 91. She was the last remaining female Spitfire pilot.

Birthplace: Quilmes, Argentina
Born: 1920 **Died:** 2012
Known For: Flying Spitfires
during World War Two

Michael Marks
Retailer

Michael Marks was born in Slonim, Russia (now Belarus) in 1859. He was born into a Polish-Jewish family and, aged about 23, moved to England to escape persecution from the Russian state. He sought out a company in Leeds that was known to employ Jewish refugees.

With hardly a penny to his name and unable to speak English, he began meeting with his fellow Jewish immigrants. In 1886, he married Hannah Cohen at the Great Synagogue on Belgrave Street, Leeds. Two years later, he met Isaac Dewhirst and borrowed £5 to set up a door-to-door sales business, selling simple clothes to small villages in Leeds. The endeavour succeeded and eventually Marks had saved enough money to open a small penny bazaar on a market stall at Leeds Kirkgate Market. Its slogan was 'Don't Ask the Price, It's a Penny.' Marks continued to expand the business and opened similar stalls across Yorkshire and Lancashire.

With the business beginning to grow, Marks recognised that he needed some assistance and, in 1894, he met a cashier by the name of Tom Spencer who invested £300 in return for half of the business. With Marks running the market stalls and Spencer managing the office and warehouse, the pair opened more stalls in Bristol, Birmingham, Cardiff, Hull, Liverpool, Middlesbrough and Sunderland. Eventually they opened a main warehouse in Manchester and expanded across the UK. In 1903, Marks & Spencer became a limited company and is known as one of Britain's major multinational retailers, specialising in clothing, homeware, and food. Today, Michael Marks's legacy can be found on almost every high street throughout the United Kingdom.

Birthplace: Slonim, Belarus
Born: 1959 **Died:** 1907
Known For: Starting
Marks & Spencer

Mo Farah
Athlete

Mo Farah, one of the greatest long-distance runners in the world, was born in Mogadishu, Somalia in 1983. With political and social tensions rife in the country, his family were forced to flee. At the age of eight, he was resettled in London without a word of English to his name. Assimilation, at least initially, was problematical. He later described his school years by saying: 'I was this African kid who looked as if he needed sorting. I ended up with a black eye.'

He soon found himself best able to articulate himself through sport. He initially harboured dreams of playing football, ideally for Arsenal, but his teachers steered him into running, his long-limbed gait ideal for the track. Aged 16, he won his first major long-distance title in the 5,000 metres at the European Athletics Junior Championships, where he was mentored by the Greek shipping magnate Sir Eddie Kulukundis. Kulukundis later covered the legal costs of Mo's naturalisation as a British citizen. He reached the 2008 Beijing Olympics, but was knocked out in the early heats. But Mo, who didn't lack self-belief, vowed that he would do better in four years' time.

At the 2012 London Olympics, Mo took gold in both the 5,000 and 10,000 metres, making him one of the best loved British athletes of the modern era. In 2013, he was appointed a CBE for services to athletics. At the Rio Olympics in 2016, he again won gold in both the 10,000 and the 5,000 metres. After retiring from the track, he continued to run competitively and over recent years has been a regular fixture at the Great North Run and the London Marathon. In 2017, he was knighted. He has used his profile to raise money for many charities, most notably the London Organising Committee of the Olympic and Paralympic Games and Marathon Kids.

Birthplace: Mogadishu, Somalia
Born: 1983
Known For: Winning four
Olympic gold medals

Mona Hatoum
Artist

Mona Hatoum was born in 1952 in Beirut, Lebanon. From a young age she loved to draw and later studied graphic design at Beirut University College. In 1975, her life was uprooted by the outbreak of Lebanon's long Civil War. On a trip to London, she decided to stay and make Britain her home to avoid the conflict. She studied at the Byam Shaw School of Art and UCL Slade School of Fine Art where she channelled her interest in human struggles into her art. Her artwork often uses the human body to depict oppression, violence, sexuality and the psychological effect of being displaced. Its beauty stands in stark counterpoint to the darkness of the subject matter, creating a visceral response within viewers.

Initially, Mona specialised in using performance art to comment on political and gender conflicts. She then focussed on physical objects and installations. One of her many notable pieces, featured in London's Tate Modern, was Grate Divide, an enlarged kitchen grating utensil perhaps used to depict the damaging effect of separation between peoples caused by political alienation or borders.

Mona's work, both performance and installations, have been put on display across the world, including at the Pompidou Centre in Paris, The New Museum of Contemporary Art in New York, and the Museum of Contemporary Art in Sydney. Her contribution to art and sculpture in Britain was recognised by Tate Modern when it staged an exhibition of her work in 2016.

Birthplace: Beirut, Lebanon
Born: 1952
Known For: Making
challenging art

Montague Burton
Retailer

Born in 1885 in Kaunas Province in modern-day Lithuania, Meshe Osinsky fled to England in 1900 to escape anti-Semitic pogroms that were ravaging the Russian Empire. Meshe spoke very little English when he arrived aged 15, in Cheetham Hill, Yorkshire. He had a strong desire to build a better life for himself. He is believed to have worked as a pedlar before setting up his own business with £100 borrowed from a relative. By 1904, he owned and ran a small clothing shop in Chesterfield. He opened more shops, specialising in pre-made clothing for working men. Nine years after his arrival in the UK, he married Sophie Amelia Marks, and they moved to Sheffield and had four children.

After taking British citizenship, Meshe opened a new shop which he named Burton & Burton. The firm offered bespoke tailoring where customers could choose their own fabrics and designs. One of Meshe's insights was: 'Good clothes develop a man's self-respect.' By 1929, Burton & Burton had 400 shops, factories, and mills and his company was listed on the London Stock Exchange. During World War Two, it produced a quarter of British military uniforms and a third of demobilisation suits. A year later, Meshe renamed the business Montague Burton, the Tailor of Taste Ltd, and personally assumed the name Montague Burton.

Sir Montague Burton died in 1952 and was buried in Leeds. By that time, Montague Burton was the largest tailor in the world.

Birthplace: Kaunas Province, Lithuania
Born: 1885 **Died:** 1952
Known For: Founding one of Britain's largest clothes chains.

Moses Montefiore
Banker

Moses Montefiore was born in 1784 in Leghorn, Tuscany, to a prosperous Jewish family with roots across Europe. As a young child, he was educated in London, but did not complete his schooling when his family ran out of money. He went to work at a tea wholesaler, and later in a counting house in the City of London. He married Judith Cohen, whose sister Henriette – fortuitously for Moses – wed the head of the Rothschild banking family, Nathan Mayer Rothschild. Moses became a business partner, working on the London Stock Exchange, and earned enough money to retire in his late 30s.

He devoted the rest of his life and his fortune to helping others. Many of his efforts were spent campaigning to protect Jews, in Britain and abroad. He was President of the Board of Deputies of British Jews for 39 years, from 1835 to 1874, the longest ever tenure. He also lobbied the Khedive of Egypt, the Sultan of the Ottoman Empire and Tsar Nicholas I of Russia to end persecution of Jews within their borders.

He was also a social reformer and he is mentioned in the works of Charles Dickens, George Eliot and James Joyce for his public initiatives. In 1837, he was knighted by Queen Victoria. His 100th birthday in 1884 was celebrated as an international event by Jews across the world. He died nine months later, in July 1885. His life and work has been commemorated across the world, including in the Kent seaside town of Ramsgate, where he bought a country estate and which is home to the Montefiore Synagogue.

Birthplace: Livorno, Italy
Born: 1784 **Died:** 1885
Known For: Campaigning
against religious persecution

Nasser Hussain
Cricketer

Cricketing legend Nasser Hussain was born in Chennai, India, in 1968. He is of dual heritage, with an English mother and an Indian father. He gravitated towards cricket from a young age, and played with his brothers where his talent for bowling was evident. In 1975, he and his family moved to Britain, where they settled in East London. Here, Nassar continued to play cricket for local teams, and later played for England Schools, alongside such future stars as Mike Atherton, Mark Ramprakash, Graham Gooch, Graham Thorpe and Trevor Ward.

In 1990, he made his first Test Match debut for England against the West Indies. He secured his position on the team in 1996 after winning the Man of the Match against India. Three years later, he succeeded Alec Stewart as captain and won four Test seasons in a row, as England rose to third in the International Test rankings. His highest Test score was a lofty 207. At 36, he stepped down from professional cricket, having played 96 test matches and 88 one-day international games, across which he scored 8,096 runs. The former chief sportswriter of *The Times*, Simon Barnes, described him as 'perhaps the finest captain to hold the office.'

Confirmation of the affection and admiration in which he was held was sealed almost immediately upon retirement: he was swiftly installed on the commentary team for Sky Sports alongside other former England greats Bob Willis, David Gower, and Ian Botham. In 2004, he published his autobiography, *Playing with Fire*, which won Best Autobiography at the 2005 British Sports Book Awards. In 2011, he played himself in a Bollywood movie, *Patiala House*.

Birthplace: Chennai, India
Born: 1968
Known For: Captaining the
England cricket team

Oscar Nemon
Sculptor

Oscar Nemon's life was shaped by the rise of anti-Semitism. Born in Croatia in 1906 to a Jewish family, he grew up in Osijek on the outskirts of the Austro-Hungarian Empire. As a teenager, he developed an interest in art. He was fascinated by sculpture and exhibited his early work while fulfilling private commissions. He moved to Vienna as a young man but anti-Semitism made it impossible for him to gain a formal education, so he moved to Brussels in 1925. He studied sculpture and specialised in modelling in clay directly from life. In 1930, he held his first major exhibition, displaying a unique style that resulted in commissions from Belgium's royal family and politicians and Sigmund Freud.

By 1938, anti-Semitism had become so virulent that he was forced to travel to England. His mother and brother were unable to escape and perished in the Holocaust. He and his wife Patricia settled in Oxford and had three children. In 1951, he was introduced to Winston Churchill and his wife, Clementine, who was so impressed by his work that she commissioned him to sculpt her husband as a gift for the Queen. The prime minister and the artist got on so well that Oscar modelled more than a dozen public sculptures of Churchill, including one that stands outside the House of Commons. He also sculpted Queen Elizabeth, Margaret Thatcher, and Princess Diana.

Oscar was famed for his charm and ability to evoke expression on the faces of his subjects, from laughter to grimace. He incorporated these characteristics into their portrayals, creating the distinctive works which still stand in streets, squares and parks around London and the world.

Birthplace: Osijek, Croatia
Born: 1906 **Died:** 1985
Known For: Sculpting
Winston Churchill

Parveen Kumar
Doctor

Parveen Kumar was born in 1942 in Lahore, in British India, now Pakistan. As a child, she aspired to become a doctor and later moved to London to study medicine at St Bartholomew's Hospital Medical College, where she joined its gastroenterology team. She specialised in disease of the small bowel, particularly coeliac disease, which is caused by a reaction to gluten and affects around one in 100 people. While treating the public in the National Health Service, she set up the first MSc course on gastroenterology in the UK.

As director of postgraduate medical education for Barts and the London School of Medicine and Dentistry, Parveen remembered how she had found the standard student textbook on gastroenterology boring. She decided to write a new doctor-friendly guide to clinical medicine, with the help of her colleague Mike Clark. Their work, *Kumar and Clark's Clinical Medicine*, is now the new standard medical textbook and is indispensable to doctors and students worldwide. Ranging from diabetes to psychology, it was described by the BMA Medical Book Awards judges as 'stunning in its breadth and ease of use'.

Parveen served as president of the British Medical Association and as president of the Royal Society of Medicine. The British Medical Association awarded her a gold medal. In 2017, she was made Dame Parveen Kumar. Two years later, she received the Award for Outstanding Contribution to Health from the *British Medical Journal*.

Birthplace: Lahore, Pakistan
Born: 1942
Known For: Writing *Kumar and Clark's Clinical Medicine*

Peter Porter
Poet

Peter Porter, an Australian-British poet, was born in Brisbane in 1929 into a middle-class family. He was an only child. When his mother passed away unexpectedly in 1938 when he was nine, he was devastated. His father, a salesman, enrolled him in boarding school, where he discovered a fondness for literature and writing. Despite his academic capabilities, his father could not afford to send him to university. Instead, Peter began reporting minor news stories for *The Courier-Mail* in Brisbane. He found the job so tedious that he decided to take a steamboat to England in 1951.

He settled in London and joined a contemporary poetry society called The Group, where he nurtured his talent for poetry. His poems reflected his vast knowledge of history, art and culture, while providing a candid and often humorous snapshot of everyday life. *Once Bitten Twice Bitten,* the first of many collections, was published in 1961. In 1983, he won the Duff Cooper Prize for Collected Poems, followed five years later by the Whitbread Prize for Poetry. In 2001, he was made Poet in Residence at the Royal Albert Hall, and a year later received the Queen's gold medal for poetry.

Through his career, he worked as a resident writer at a number of leading universities and edited more than 20 collections of poetry. He died in 2010 following a battle with liver cancer. *The Australian Book Review* renamed its award for a new poem the Peter Porter Poetry Prize.

Birthplace: Brisbane, Australia
Born: 1929 **Died:** 2010
Known For: Composing
clever and satirical poems

Prince Albert
Royal consort

Prince Albert of Saxe-Coburg and Gotha was born in 1819 at Schloss Rosenau in Germany, the second son of Ernest III, Duke of Saxe-Coburg-Saalfeld, a German dynasty connected to many of Europe's royal families. His uncle, Leopold I, hoped he would marry the future Queen of England, Victoria, and in 1840, the marriage took place. At first, Albert was unpopular with the British public who suspected he had married for money. In reality, he was devoted to his wife and became her private secretary and adviser.

Albert had a keen interest in public causes. He supported raising the working age for children. He campaigned for the abolition of slavery and became president of the Society for the Extinction of Slavery. He reformed university education and became Chancellor of the University of Cambridge in 1847. In 1851, he co-organised the Great Exhibition in Hyde Park, which sought to showcase how science and industry could improve society. Charles Dickens, Charlotte Brontë, and Lewis Carroll were among the six million Britons who visited it – a quarter of the population. Albert also introduced the principle that the royal family should remain above politics, encouraging Victoria to take a politically neutral stance and abandon her Whig connections.

In 1861, he died of typhoid fever, aged 42. After his death, Queen Victoria wore black for the remaining 40 years of her life. Her grief was known across the country and the public's resentment of Albert faded. Today, his progressive views and influences are recognised as beginning a modernisation of the role of the British monarchy.

Birthplace: Schloss Rosenau, Germany
Born: 1819 **Died:** 1861
Known For: Being a progressive influence on the Royal Family

Raheem Sterling
Footballer

Before he became one of England's best footballers, Raheem Shaquille Sterling had a tough upbringing in Jamaica and Britain. His father was murdered two years after he was born in 1994. His mother decided to study for a degree in England in the hope of giving her children a better life. Raheem eventually joined her in Wembley, London, in 1999, aged five.

With his talent for dribbling, he played in the youth squad at Queens Park Rangers, but his family struggled to make ends meet. He recalled later: 'I can remember when I was a kid, there was like three or four times when I was on the bus home from training and my mum would text me a new address. And she would say: "This is where we're living now." There was a two-year period where we were moving all the time, because we couldn't afford the rent.'

He signed for Liverpool and became its youngest player to score in a competitive game. He won young player of the year two years in a row as the club challenged for the Premier League. In 2015, he signed for Manchester City. The £44 million made him one of the most expensive players in the league's history, but the real prize came when Manchester City won the Premiership in 2018-19 – the same year he was named the Football Writers' Association Footballer of the Year. He has made more than 50 appearances for England. He was a member of the team which came fourth at the 2018 World Cup, the national team's highest placing for 28 years. He has condemned racism in foreign stadiums towards England's black players and the British press for fuelling racism against black sportsmen at home.

Birthplace: Kingston, Jamaica
Born: 1994
Known For: Scoring goals for
Manchester City and England

Richard Rogers
Architect

Richard Rogers was born in Florence in 1933 into an Italian family with ancestral ties to England. When he was six years old, his father, a doctor, and his mother, an artist, moved the family to England. He started school in Leatherhead without knowing any English. He was dyslexic and struggled academically, only learning to read when he was 11. But then he found his lifelong passion when he took a foundation course at Epsom School of Art and a master's degree in architecture at Yale University in 1962.

A year later he set up his own architectural firm, Team 4, with his wife Su, another star architect Norman Foster, and his later wife Wendy Cheeseman. Richards' style was simplistic and functional and in 1971 he won a competition to design the Pompidou Centre in Paris with a new team at Piano + Rogers. While at first controversial, the 'inside out' complex – which displays its structural and mechanical work on the outside – has become a landmark of the French capital. His new firm, the Richard Rogers Partnership, has designed a string of innovative buildings, notably the Millennium Dome, Heathrow Terminal Five, the National Assembly of Wales in Britain, the European Court of Human Rights in Strasbourg, Terminal 4 of Madrid–Barajas Airport, and Tower 3 of New York's New World Trade Centre.

He advised two successive mayors of London, Ken Livingstone and Boris Johnson, on urbanism and architecture. His firm, now called Rogers Stirk Harbour + Partners, continues to design multi-billion pound projects around the world and has offices in London, Shanghai and Sydney.

Birthplace: Florence, Italy
Born: 1933
Known For: Designing the Pompidou Centre in Paris

Sake Dean Mahomed
Surgeon and Entrepreneur

Sake Dean Mahomed was born in 1759 in Patna, India, then part of the Bengal Presidency. When he was young his father died, and he was cared for by an English army captain. He subsequently joined the East India Company as a trainee surgeon. In 1782, Mahomed moved to Britain, and became the first Indian to write a published book in English, *The Travels of Dean Mahomed,* about his life in Indian cities and the culture of the time.

In 1810, he opened the Hindostanee Coffee House at 34 George Street in Mayfair, London – the first Indian restaurant in Britain. A restaurant guide mentioned that nobility enjoyed traditional hookah and Indian dishes there. In 1814, he moved to Brighton to introduce another Indian concept to Europe, shampoo. He set up an Indian Vapour Bath where he introduced the treatment of shampooing to cure diseases. The venture was successful and he became a shampooing surgeon to King George IV and William IV.

Sake went on to write a number of books on the subject but his recognition faded in the years after his death, until the poet Alamgir Hashmi took interest in his work in the 1960s and 1970s. Today, Sake is considered to be one of the most influential non-European immigrants to the West. In 2005, a green plaque was placed on 102 George Street, near where the Hindostanee Coffee House served curries to earls and barons.

Birthplace: Patna, India
Born: 1759 **Died:** 1851
Known For: Introducing the Indian restaurant to Britain

Shanta Pathak
Entrepreneur

Shanta Pandit was born in 1927 in Zanzibar, Tanzinia. She married a man from Gujarat in India, Laxmishanker Pathak, in Kenya, where they ran a small business selling sweets and samosas. In 1956, after Britain's departure from the country and the Mau Mau uprising, they settled in London. With only £5 to their name, Laxmishanker started cleaning drains for Camden Council.

Shanta was unhappy that her husband had to take a job that she felt was beneath him. She also realised that his salary was not going to support their family of eight, so she restarted their small business selling Indian sweets and samosas. It prospered and the couple opened shops in Euston and Bayswater, selling foods and ingredients to the Indian community and the growing number of Asian restaurants in London. All six Pathak children helped prepare and deliver the food. In 1962, the family had to move because of complaints from neighbours about the smell of their cooking. In Brackley, Northamptonshire, and then Lancashire, they expanded the business. Their most popular products were pickles and sauces that allowed any unskilled cook to produce tasty Indian cooking.

In 1976, Laxmishanker handed over the business to their son Kirit. Thanks to his upbringing working in their shops and his wife Meena's degree in food technology, the business grew to an annual turnover of £55 million. In 2007, the family sold Patak's to Associated British Foods, owners of Twinings tea and Silver Spoon sugar, for more than £100 million. Patak's still supplies Indian restaurants with cooking sauces and spice mixes and employs 700 people in Leigh, Lancashire. Its sauces help millions of British people to cook curries.

Birthplace: Zanzibar City,
Tanzania
Born: 1927 **Died:** 2010
Known For: Founding
Patak's curry sauces

Sislin Fay Allen
Police officer

Sislin Fay Allen, known commonly by her second name Fay, was born in Jamaica in 1939. She qualified as a nurse and moved to London in 1962, where she worked at Queen's Hospital in Croydon, specialising in geriatric medicine, while raising her two children.

After four years in Britain, she saw a newspaper advertisement recruiting men and women police trainees, and decided to apply. At the time there were only 600 police women in the whole of Britain, all of them white. Fay's friends and family warned her that she would never be given the job because she was black. She attended a selection day for the job and she was offered the role. After training she undertook her first post in Croydon, becoming the first non-white policewoman in the UK. The uniqueness of her position drew attention from the public and the media when she went on patrol. She noted that members of the public would come over and congratulate her on her position, while others would stare in wonder.

While she received no direct prejudice while on duty, the Metropolitan Police received racist letters criticising the decision to hire her. She also faced hostility from some members of her own community who saw her joining the police – who were often said to behave racistly – as a betrayal. After one year in Croydon, Fay was transferred to Scotland Yard where she worked as part of the Missing Persons Unit, before undertaking her final post in Norbury. She left the force in 1972 and relocated to Jamaica with her family, but returned to England a number of years later and settled once again in south London.

Birthplace: Jamaica
Born: 1939
Known For: Becoming the first non-white female police constable

Solly Zuckerman
Military adviser

Solomon Zuckerman was born in Cape Town in 1904. He studied medicine at university in South Africa, before moving to England in the 1920s to complete his training. He began work as a resident anatomist at the London Zoological Society, specialising in primatology. His pioneering research on the sociology of monkeys and apes made him a leader in his field and improved our understanding of our closest animal relatives.

'Solly' remained at the Zoological Society until 1932, when he joined the staff of the University of Oxford. During nine years there, he joined Isaac Newton and Charles Darwin in being made a fellow of the Royal Society for making a significant contribution to the knowledge of natural sciences. He studied human anatomy and endocrinology at Yale and London universities.

On the outbreak of World War Two, he was asked to research the effects of bombings on humans and their homes. He subsequently designed a helmet worn by civilians during air raids, the Zuckerman Helmet. He enlisted in the Royal Air Force where he became honorary captain of the special duties branch, and, later, scientific director of the British Bombing Survey Unit. Using his extensive knowledge of the impact of bombings, he advised on the strategies for the D-Day Landings. When World War Two ended, he became chief scientific advisor to the British government. He was awarded a life peerage in 1971, the same year his autobiography, *From Apes to Warlords,* was published. He died at his home in London in 1993, aged 88.

Birthplace: Cape Town,
South Africa
Born: 1904   **Died:** 1993
Known For: Advising the Allies
on the D-Day landings

Stelios Haji-Ioannou
Entrepreneur

Stelios Haji-Ioannou, the uncrowned king of the budget airline, was born in Athens in 1967, to a wealthy family (his father was a shipping tycoon). After attending secondary school in Greece, he arrived in the UK to study at the London School of Economics and Cass Business School. At 20, he received a figure believed to be £30 million from his father to ease his passage into adulthood. He used the money to set up Stelmar Shipping.

He subsequently experimented with a no-frills travel company, easyJet, in 1995 with a pitch of lowering the cost of air fare for ordinary people. Inaugural flights flew between London and Scotland, but the company quickly grew as it became evident that travellers would accept less attention to customer service in exchange for cheap airline tickets. EasyJet became one of Europe's largest airlines, making holiday destinations more accessible.

Today, easyJet employs over 10,000 people and makes over half a billion flights annually. Stelios has experimented with the brand, launching Internet cafes, cheap hotels and car hire. For a time, he was very much the public face of his brand in much the same way Richard Branson is with Virgin. Outside of his myriad business ventures, he has taken an interest in politics and charitable causes. He established the Stelios Philanthropic Foundation to help support various charities in the UK, Greece and Cyprus. In 2006, he was knighted for services to entrepreneurship.

Birthplace: Athens, Greece
Born: 1967
Known For: Starting the
low-cost airline easyJet

Stephanie 'Steve' Shirley
Entrepeneur

Vera Buchthal was born in 1933 in Dortmund, Germany, into a Jewish family. Aged five, she and her brother escaped Nazi Germany on Sir Nicholas Winton's Kindertransport. She was placed with a foster family where she learned enough English to attend school. At 18, she became a British citizen and changed her name to Stephanie Brook.

In the 1950s, Stephanie began working with computers, writing code at the Post Office Research Station, while taking a degree in mathematics at night school. The computer industry was male-dominated and chauvinistic, and she later recalled 'being fondled, being pushed against the wall.' In 1962, Stephanie married a physicist, Derek Shirley, and set up a women-only software business, Freelance Programmers, at their dining table with just £6. When her letters to potential clients went unanswered, she changed her name to Steve – and began getting replies. She sold F1 International, the successor to Freelance Programmers, for an estimated £150 million. It later became the British technology and outsourcing company Xansa Plc.

Despite a thriving business career, her private life was touched by tragedy: her son Giles was severely autistic and died as a young adult. In 1986, she set up and donated much of her wealth to the Shirley Foundation, a trust fund that supports autism charities. She retired in 1993 to devote her time to those causes. So far she has given away £68 million of her wealth. She puts her generosity down to her experiences as a child refugee.

Birthplace: Dortmund, Germany
Born: 1933
Known For: Beating sexism
in a male-dominated industry

Stuart Hall
Academic

Stuart Hall was born in 1932 in Kingston, Jamaica, into a middle-class family of African, British, Portuguese-Jewish and Indian descent. This 'home of hybridity,' as he described it, spurred his interest in the politics of diversity. He was awarded a Rhodes Scholarship to study literature at Merton College, Oxford, and arrived in Britain as a part of the Windrush generation. Energised by the Suez Crisis and the Soviet invasion of Hungary, he became involved in *Universities and Left Review*, a left-leaning academic journal.

After successfully co-authoring a book, *The Popular Arts*, about the importance of analysing film as entertainment, he worked as a research fellow at the Centre for Contemporary Cultural Studies at the University of Birmingham, later becoming its director. His authored articles dramatically increased the popularity of cultural studies, earning him a job as Professor of Sociology at the Open University.

Among his wide output, much of its grounded in his desire for racial equality, he developed the encoding/decoding model of communication, worked on studies that revealed racial prejudice in the media, and sought to understand black identity in post-colonial Britain. All of his essays, books, articles and films were in some way dedicated to explaining and understanding British society and culture. In 2005, he was elected Fellow of the British Academy. He died in 2014, aged 82, by which time he was widely known as the 'godfather of multiculturalism'. The Stuart Hall Foundation spreads his legacy by arranging scholarships and fellowships for individuals who seek to change the cultural and political landscape.

Birthplace: Kingston, Jamaica
Born: 1932 **Died:** 2014
Known For: Starting
British Cultural Studies

TS Eliot
Poet

Thomas Stearns Eliot was born in 1888 in Missouri, United States. From a young age he could not play much with other children because of a congenital double hernia, which meant that he spent a lot of time reading. He developed an obsessive love of literature and began writing his own poetry at the age of 14. He studied at Harvard College and worked at a number of prominent universities until he moved to Paris in 1910 and, four years later, took up a scholarship at the University of Oxford.

The move to Britain had a profound effect on Thomas for a number of reasons. Firstly, he met Ezra Pound, an American literary figure who influenced Thomas to pursue writing as a career. The second was his failed marriage to Vivienne Haigh-Wood, out of which came his poem *The Waste Land*, now recognised as one of the greatest poems of the 20th century. In 1927, he became a British citizen. His poems, plays and literary criticism gained him the title of one of the 20th Century's major poets. Among his famous works are *The Love Song of J Alfred Prufrock, The Hollow Men, Murder in the Cathedral,* and *The Cocktail Party. Old Possum's Book of Practical Cats,* a collection of whimsical poems, later inspired the musical *Cats.* In 1945, he was awarded the Nobel Prize in Literature for his contribution to poetry. He died at his home in London in 1965.

During his life and thereafter, his work has been immensely influential, touching not only those studying English literature but also capturing the attention and imaginations of successive generations.

Birthplace: St. Louis, USA
Born: 1888 **Died:** 1965
Known For: Writing some of the
20th Century's best poetry

Tessa Sanderson
Athlete

Tessa Sanderson was born in 1956 in St Elizabeth, Jamaica, of Ghanaian ancestry. Her parents relocated to Wolverhampton in England. She stayed behind to be raised by her grandmother, until she was sent for and reunited with her parents. A keen athlete during her UK school years, Tessa's prowess with the javelin was evident from a young age. By 1972, she was the English Schools Intermediate Champion and made her international debut shortly after.

She represented Britain in her first Olympic Games in Montréal in 1976 at the age of 20 – the youngest competitor to make the final. She made the Olympic final again in Moscow four years later, and entered a golden period in her career. At the 1984 Los Angeles Games, she became one of the first British women athletes to win an Olympic gold. She won gold at the Commonwealth Games in Edinburgh two years later and again at the Commonwealth Games in Auckland in 1990. In all, she represented Britain at six Olympics. She set many national and international javelin records, which affirmed her position as a sporting force, and an inspiration for British female athletes who followed in her wake.

After retiring from athletics, she took on the role of vice chairman of Sport England and set up the Tessa Sanderson Foundation, a charity and academy dedicated to making sport more accessible to children and young people. She helped organise the first Newham 10k run in 2009, giving participants the opportunity to run through the Olympic Park. The event was so successful that it continues to be staged annually, and has inspired similar runs across the capital.

Birthplace: St. Elizabeth Parish, Jamaica
Born: 1956
Known For: Winning gold at the 1984 Olympics

Trevor McDonald
Journalist and Newscaster

Trevor McDonald was born in Trinidad in 1939, and first worked as a broadcast journalist in the Caribbean during the 1960s. He moved to London to work as a producer for the BBC and became ITN's first black reporter in 1973. As well as helming the 10 o'clock news, he was increasingly dispatched around the world to interview leading political and cultural figures. He was the first journalist to interview Nelson Mandela following Mandela's liberation from Robben Island in 1990. He also interviewed Saddam Hussein and Colonel Gaddafi. Gaddafi was reported to be so impressed by him that he offered him a job.

In 1992, he became ITV's main news anchor, increasingly respected by his peers and the viewing public for an assured style many described as avuncular. He presented the ITV news in its various guises as *News At Ten*, *The ITV Evening News* and, later, *ITV News* at 10.30pm. After more than 30 years at the channel he presented his last late-night night bulletin in December 2005. That is, until 2008, when his gravitas and charm made him a natural candidate to be coaxed out of retirement to relaunch *News at Ten* with Julie Etchingham. He has continued to present TV programmes since, hosting a succession of investigative documentaries from around the world on wide-ranging topics such as the Mafia, death row and Scotland Yard.

Made an OBE in 1992 for services to journalism, he was knighted seven years later, and awarded the BAFTA fellowship in 2011.

Birthplace: San Fernando, Trinidad and Tobago
Born: 1939
Known For: Presenting ITV News for decades

Valerie Amos
Lawyer and politician

Valerie Amos was born in 1954 in Guyana, South America. She attended secondary school in London and universities in Warwick, Birmingham and East Anglia. Throughout the 1980s, she worked in local government in London, where she campaigned to improve employment rights for part-time workers and women. In 1989, she continued her work against sex discrimination as chief executive of the Equal Opportunities Commission.

In 1997, she entered the House of Lords, and, a year later, joined Tony Blair's Labour government as a junior foreign minister. In 2003, she became the first black woman to serve in the Cabinet when she took the job of Secretary of State for International Development. Within six months, she was promoted to Leader of the House of Lords, managing the government's business in the second chamber.

After briefly serving as British High Commissioner to Australia, she joined the UN as Under-Secretary-General for Humanitarian Affairs and Emergency Relief Coordinator. In 2005, she became Director of SOAS University of London, becoming the first black woman to run a British university. In 2009, she and her sister, Colleen Amos OBE, set up the Amos Bursary in an attempt to end the under representation of young British men of African and Caribbean descent in higher education and the professions. In 2019, the University of Oxford announced that she was becoming the first female master of University College – and the first black head of an Oxford college, smashing yet another glass ceiling in a life dedicated to helping others rise.

Birthplace: Georgetown, Guyana
Born: 1954
Known For: Being the first black woman to serve in the Cabinet

Venkatraman Ramakrishnan
Biologist

Venkatraman Ramakrishnan was born in 1952 in Tamil Nadu, India, to a family of prominent scientists. He earned a degree in physics and moved to the United States, where he studied philosophy and biology. He spent years at Yale University and at the Brookhaven National Laboratory researching the ribosome, the protein machine in every living cell that brings DNA to life.

In 1999, he moved to Britain to work at the Laboratory of Molecular Biology in Cambridge. There, he and his colleagues, Thomas Steitz and Ada Yonath, made a breakthrough in understanding how the ribosome worked. Many existing antibiotics work by disabling the ribosome, meaning that Venkatraman's work could help develop new drugs to replace ones losing their effectiveness. In 2009, Venkatraman and his colleagues were awarded the Nobel Prize for Chemistry for their discovery. The Nobel Foundation explained: 'An understanding of the ribosome's innermost workings is important for a scientific understanding of life. This knowledge can be put to a practical and immediate use... to develop new antibiotics, directly assisting the saving of lives and decreasing humanity's suffering.'

Venkatraman was made a Fellow of the Royal Society and elected a Member of the European Molecular Biology Organization. In 2012, he was knighted and awarded the Sir Hans Krebs Medal for his services to biology. In 2015, he was elected President of the Royal Society – the first Indian-born individual to lead the UK's foremost scientific organisation. His success enabled him to reconnect with India where he also won a number of high-ranking awards and recognitions. He continues to work in Britain.

Birthplace: Tamil Nadu, India
Born: 1952
Known For: Making a discovery
that has boosted antibiotics

Vera Atkins
Wartime spy

Vera Maria Rosenberg was born in 1908 in Galati, Romania into an upper-class German-Jewish family. Her half British mother's maiden name was Atkins. Vera spent much of her young life moving between European cities attending schools in London, Paris and Lausanne, returning occasionally to her father's large estate in Romania. When the Nazis invaded Germany in 1940, she moved to the UK, where she became a British agent.

In 1939, she helped smuggle the Polish code-breakers who had broken Germany's Enigma machine into Romania and then to the West where they passed on their crucial expertise. In 1941, she joined the Special Operations Executive, an organisation set up by Winston Churchill to conduct espionage, sabotage and reconnaissance in occupied Europe. Her first position was as a secretary, but she quickly became deputy to Colonel Maurice Buckmaster, leader of the French section. She was responsible for recruiting and deploying agents into occupied France, and taught them how to assimilate into French society. She would wave them goodbye at the airfield where they would depart to France, many never to return.

After the war, she spent time in France and Germany searching for agents that had been reported missing in action, most of whom had died in concentration camps. On her return to Britain, she was part of the team that investigated war crimes, interrogating high profile Nazis, including Rudolf Höss, the ex-commandant of Auschwitz-Birkenau. She was demobilised in 1947. She went to work for the United Nations Educational, Scientific and Cultural Organization, becoming its director in 1952. In 1997, she was appointed CBE. She died in 2000. She was 92.

Birthplace: Galati, Romania
Born: 1908 **Died:** 2000
Known For: Deploying British
agents in World War Two

Violette Szabo
Wartime spy

Violette Bushell was born in Paris in 1921, to a French mother and English father. They had four sons and Violette. She was a free-spirited, energetic child who enjoyed sports and physical activity and earned a reputation as a tomboy. The Great Depression in the 1930s forced the Szabos to move to London, where Violette spent much of her young life in Brixton.

During World War Two, Violette joined the Women's Land Army to help with food production. Her new husband, Etienne Szabo, a French soldier, was killed in battle shortly after the birth of their daughter. She volunteered to join the Special Operations Executive, bolstered by her fluency in French and English and aptitude at shooting. She passed the arduous training and was tasked with collecting intelligence and delivering messages to allies behind enemy lines. On her first mission in April 1944, Violette discovered that many French resistance workers had been captured by the Gestapo and successfully relayed this information to the SOE. As a result, the British learned much more about the Rouen area and its resistance to the advancing Nazi forces.

During her second SOE mission, two months later, Violette, then 23, was travelling to meet her counterpart in Limoges in southern France when she was stopped at a checkpoint by the Gestapo. Following a shoot-out, she was arrested, deported and tortured at Ravensbruck concentration camp in Germany. She was executed at Ravensbruck on 5 February 1945, three months before the end of the war in Europe. She was posthumously awarded the George Cross in 1946, only the second woman ever to receive the honour. France's Croix de Guerre was awarded a year later.

Birthplace: Paris, France
Born: 1921 **Died:** 1945
Known For: Working
with the French resistance

William Butement
Scientist

William Butement was born in 1904 in Masterton, New Zealand. His father was a physician and surgeon. When William was eight, he and his family moved to Australia, and – a year later – to London. William graduated with a degree in physics from the University of London and took a job at the War Office's signals research base in Woolwich, London.

During his time at the Signals Experimental Establishment, he made a breakthrough and developed equipment that could detect ships. The War Office was not interested, until another team at the Air Ministry began working on something similar. He joined that team and helped create many new devices, including a coastal defence system that could detect enemy aircraft and ships. His initial ship-detecting equipment was Britain's first step towards developing radar, which helped detect Luftwaffe planes early and win the Battle of Britain. He also played a significant part in the development of the proximity fuse, a device that automatically detonated when the missile closed in on its target. He also invented the forerunner of the Wireless Station 10, which allowed soldiers to communicate wirelessly on the battlefield during World War Two. His inventions made a significant contribution to the Allies winning the war.

After the war, he returned to Australia, but continued to be involved in British military science and helped to test British nuclear weapons in Australia. In 1946, he was made an OBE and, in 1959, a CBE. He died in Melbourne in 1990.

Birthplace: Masterton, New Zealand
Born: 1904 **Died:** 1990
Known For: Developing radar in World War Two

Yasmin Qureshi
Politician and barrister

Yasmin Qureshi was born in 1963 in Gujrat City, Pakistan, the youngest of three children. Her family moved to Britain when she was nine, and settled in Watford. After taking a degree in law at London South Bank University, she sat her exams to become a barrister. She joined the Crown Prosecution Service, where she developed expertise in complex criminal cases. She later headed the criminal legal section of the United Nations mission in Kosovo, dealing with people trafficking and domestic violence. Between 2004 and 2008, she was human rights advisor to London's mayor, Ken Livingstone.

But she decided to go into politics and she was selected as the prospective parliamentary candidate for Bolton South East in Lancashire. She moved her barristers chambers from London to Manchester to work closer to the constituency. In 2010, she was finally elected. Alongside fellow parliamentary newcomers Rushanara Ali and Shabana Mahmood, she was the first female Muslim MP.

During her time in the House of Commons, Yasmin served on the Foreign affairs, Home Affairs, and Justice select committees. She campaigned on issues including the NHS, prisons, pharmacies, crime, transport, and the courts. She was one of the leading voices for making upskirting a criminal offence, which finally became law in 2019. She also spoke out against the murder of Rohingya Muslims in Myanmar. In 2014, she was awarded Politician of the Year award at the British Muslim Awards.

Birthplace: Gujrat City, Pakistan
Born: 1963
Known For: Campaigning
for human rights

Yvonne Thompson
Entrepreneur

Yvonne Thompson's entrepreneurial spirit manifested itself from an early age. Born in Guyana, South America, she moved to Britain with her parents in 1961, settling in Battersea, London. She faced both racism and sexism at school, and then again during the early part of her career when she worked for a high street bank. So she decided to set up her own PR company, ASAP Communications, which specialised in representing black music artists, the first of its kind. She went on to found Britain's first black radio station, Choice FM, known today as Capital XTRA, which reached an estimated 1.8 million people in Britain.

Later on in her career, she founded the European Federation of Black Women Business Owners, which continues to operate today. Frequently referred to as 'Britain's first black self-made woman millionaire', she has used her position, wealth and influence, to champion equality in the workplace for women and minorities.

Her dedication to serving small businesses has earned her an honorary doctorate from London Metropolitan University, and she now holds the title Dr Yvonne Thompson. In 2001, she received the European Women of Achievement Award, and two years later was appointed a CBE for her services to black and ethnic minority advancements in business. Her impact has been felt around the world. In Houston, Texas, in 2004, the city mayor declared 4 January as 'Yvonne Thompson Day' in recognition of her achievements.

Birthplace: Guyana,
South America
Born: 1955
Known For: Founding
radio station Choice FM

Zaha Hadid
Architect

Zaha Hadid was born in Iraq in 1950 to a wealthy family familiar with business and art: her father was an industrialist and her mother an artist. She attended boarding schools in England and Switzerland, before studying mathematics at the American University of Beirut, then architecture at the Architectural Association School of Architecture in London.

In 1980, after becoming a naturalised citizen of the United Kingdom, she founded her own firm, Zaha Hadid Architects. For years, her swooping, ambitious designs were so striking and unusual they featured in design journals, but were never built. The first design that was actually built was a fire station at Weil am Rhein, Germany, in 1991. After that, there was no stopping her. She pushed the boundaries of design in Britain and internationally with the construction of bold private and public buildings, including arts and science centres and bridges. Known as the queen of curves, she conjured up the wavy-roofed Riverside Museum in Glasgow and the sleek fly-away London Aquatics Centre for the 2012 Olympics – inspired by the 'fluid geometry of water in movement'.

Shortly after she won the UK's Stirling Prize twice for buildings in Rome and London, *Forbes Magazine* described her as one of the world's most powerful women. She was the first female recipient of the Royal Institute of British Architect's Royal Gold Medal. In 2016, she became unwell while staying in Miami. She had a massive heart attack and died. She was 65. Zaha Hadid Architects remains one of Britain's leading architectural practices.

Birthplace: Baghdad, Iraq
Born: 1950 **Died:** 2016
Known For: Designing
the London Aquatic Centre

Birthplace:
Born:
Known For: